My L
My Legacy

*Turning the Unexpected into
a Lifetime of Cherished Memories*

A Memoir

By Kefa Oduor Tuju

 FriesenPress

Suite 300 - 990 Fort St
Victoria, BC, V8V 3K2
Canada

www.friesenpress.com

Copyright © 2020 by Kefa Oduor Tuju
First Edition — 2020

All rights reserved.

Written by Kefa Oduor Tuju and Christine Wangui Oduor

Edited by Susan Braid

No part of this publication may be reproduced in any form, or by any means, electronic or mechanical, including photocopying, recording, or any information browsing, storage, or retrieval system, without permission in writing from FriesenPress.

ISBN
978-1-5255-7714-7 (Hardcover)
978-1-5255-7715-4 (Paperback)
978-1-5255-7716-1 (eBook)

1. BIOGRAPHY & AUTOBIOGRAPHY, PERSONAL MEMOIRS

Distributed to the trade by The Ingram Book Company

DEDICATION

This memoir is dedicated to my wonderful sons,
Jonathan and Matthew Oduor
and to my lovely wife Christine Wangui Oduor,
as a sign of my love to you.

I also dedicate this to my amazing mother,
Mary Odiyo, who has been a strong pillar
and model of peace, resilience and endurance.

SPECIAL THANKS

I wish to appreciate and give special mention to friends who have worked tirelessly to make the completion of this memoir possible.

Christine Oduor – who burnt the midnight oil and spent tireless nights typing on my behalf, given the poor mobility on my left hand.

Natalie Oliphant – who believed in my dream to write this memoir and helped to get it started.

Jim Burk, a published writer, who gave untold hours of technical input and support to publish the first e-book on Kobo.

Sue Braid for her dedicated service in editing.

Petara Panabaker who offered her photography skills at no charge to obtain our family portraits in honor of families battling cancer.

Many others who offered helpful assistance.

TABLE OF CONTENTS

Foreword	ix
Chapter 1: My Family, My Roots	1
Chapter 2: Childhood	11
Chapter 3: Early Adulthood And Career	21
Chapter 4: Courtship And Marriage	37
Chapter 5: Children	55
Chapter 6: The Move	67
Chapter 7: How I Beat Cancer	75
Chapter 8: Changes	101
Chapter 9: Reflections From A Hospice Room	107
Chapter 10: Loving Words And Thoughts From George Davison Elementary School	111
Chapter 11: Epilogue	117
Acknowledgements	155
Photo Gallery	157

FOREWORD

In Kenya, one of the greatest gifts a man can give is his legacy. A story of his life, thoughts and beliefs not only for his children, but for generations to come. Words that describe a man by the man. Words that bring his life alive long after he is gone for every generation to know and appreciate. Each man's life is a collection of stories. Some stories are positive, making us smile or laugh, even nod in recognition. Others sound cruel, painful and speak of events that cause a twinge of discomfort. This is such a life, a collection, a legacy. Questions, stories, thoughts and truths of Kefa Oduor Tuju.

CHAPTER 1:

MY FAMILY, MY ROOTS

I was the sixth child of nine children born to my mother and father. My father, Henry Odiyo Tuju (deceased in 2017), had two wives. Polygamy was widespread then and was an accepted cultural practice in my Luo community in Kenya. In fact, having more than one wife was considered prestigious and it was a sign of being wealthy. Therefore, we did not find it strange to have two mothers around as we grew up.

Polygamy was complemented by having as many children as possible. My father had twenty-two children in total. My mother Mary Ogola was blessed with nine children while my stepmother, Rispa Odiyo, was blessed with thirteen children. As I write this, three of the twenty-two children are now deceased.

My father tried his best to keep the two families together. In the village, he ensured that there was a house built for each of his wives all in the same compound. We could walk freely back and forth and in and out of either of the houses.

However, this arrangement was not possible in the city of Nairobi where housing and life was expensive. My dad, who worked for the Kenya Railways full-time, was given the benefit of a house in the city of Nairobi—but only one house—which meant that both wives could not fit in the small two-bedroomed unit. According to our custom my mother, as the first wife, was required to live in the village while my stepmom lived in the city of Nairobi with my dad.

My mom and late dad at our upcountry home in Asembo, Kenya. October 2014

My siblings on my mom's side include, in order of birth, Raphael Tuju, Paul Anyango (deceased), Ruth Adhiambo, Esther Awino, Collin Odiyo(deceased), myself, Saphern Ngala, Betty Achieng Wicker and Caleb Buore.

My step-siblings, in birth order, are Allan Tuju, Tito Aruwa, Dan Odhiambo, Roselyn Odiyo, Benta, Sila Abuoga, Ida Tuju, Omondi Tuju, Loise Akinyi, Carol Oduor, Pascal Nengo, Leakey Tuju and Moses Obulo Altogether, we were large enough to make two soccer teams!

I remember that as I grew up, I never saw my father smoking cigarettes or drinking any alcohol. He encouraged all of us to follow his example. He also taught me to work hard in school. I think my dad was generally happy with his life aside from the fact that he struggled with diabetes for most of his adult life. I feel he was also content because he could sit at the verandah at any of his wives' houses and he would be fed his favorite meals.

I don't know much about my grandparents because they had passed away by the time I was born. My maternal grandparents were not known as we came to learn that our mother was adopted at a young age. She was brought up by a family in the Kisii community. Coming from an oral culture, information on my grandparents is scanty.

My father came from a large family as well. My paternal grandfather was called Tuju and his wife was Obulo Nyar Msunga. My father had several brothers and sisters. He was the firstborn. His brothers were David Adem, James Tuju aka Ali, and Awour Tuju. All my uncles lived in the neighborhood in the village.

His sisters were Aunts Saulina, Doris, Roseline and Janet, who was the youngest of the siblings. Aunt Janet lived in Nairobi as she worked as a nurse at one of the provincial hospitals. She loved us dearly and has always been a great encouragement to my family.

In my Luo community, as young boys became teenagers, they were expected to move out of their parents' house and build their own little 'house' dubbed 'simba'. This house was to be built within the homestead and one was expected to spend at least one night in it before one could go out and buy or build a house anywhere else in the country. The bathroom was out back as it was meant to be a temporary arrangement. Teen girls were not allowed in the boys 'simba'. For a long time, I never saw the point of building this 'simba' while a teen or young adult. I considered having to build a 'simba' a waste of money because I would rarely go to the village. The few times that I did, I found it was easier to get accommodation with a sibling or in a hotel close by.

My beautiful mother Mary

My late dad – Henry Odiyo

My mom – Mary Ogola

My dad with some of my siblings

My mom, Ngala, Betty and myself to the right

My stepmom Rispa with some of my siblings

My extended family gathered together in Nairobi, Kenya, 2014

CHAPTER 2:

CHILDHOOD

Early Childhood

I was born in a small town called Bondo, in Nyanza Province, Kenya on September 13th, 1971. My mom told me that she had a very difficult labor and birth with me. She had some complications, but I am grateful that she came through safely despite it all. She said my eldest brother Raphael struggled to get her a ride to the hospital for my delivery. In those days, only a handful of people in the rural village had vehicles and public transport was scarce and unreliable. It was a miracle that Raphael, who was just shy of thirteen years, was able to flag down a vehicle to address this emergency. She was able to reach the nearest hospital and get medical attention for my safe delivery.

For the first five years of my life I lived in a village called Asembo. Village life was very simple. We did not have the luxuries of modern, everyday life. I recall that we had no bathroom for the children to take a bath. We used a metal pail for bathing, which was done outside during the day when the sun was up. We did not have the luxury of towels, and with Bondo reaching temperatures between 25 and 30 degrees Celsius, we dried out in the sun pretty fast. The toilet was usually separate from the bathroom (shower room) and both of these were out back. We did not have running water in the house. The water we used was collected through a gutter from the rusty tin-sheet roof of the house. We left the water out in the sun until it was lukewarm.

My mother would bathe us children in the open and let us dry out in the sun before dressing us.

As small children, life in the village was fun. There were always many other children to play with. We ran around the open fields, we made soccer balls by tying up lots of plastic. We climbed trees and loved the mango and guava trees in particular because of the fruit that we ate freely. There was never a dull moment. We played with the chickens that we reared in our compound. I recall scattering maize on the ground for the chickens to feed on. We particularly enjoyed molding familiar animals from mud which we then used as toys.

Primary School

My father wanted all his children to have a good education. He preferred that all our primary schooling would be in the city of Nairobi as opposed to the rural upcountry schools. Nairobi City was about 400 km from my village. My turn to go to the big city finally came when I was five years old. I was so excited and could hardly sit still. My mother got me ready for the long journey. She bathed me out in the open in the metal pail as usual, helped me get dressed and packed up my few clothes in a small bag. We departed to Kisumu town, which was about 40 km from our village. From there we boarded the train to Nairobi City.

As we arrived at the train station in Nairobi, I could not help but notice the number of tall buildings. The city was extremely busy with many people, carts, cars and buses. We took a public vehicle to my dad's house in Nairobi West. He was lucky to be housed by his employer, Kenya Railways, in a large wooden house with two bedrooms and a store where we kept our cartons of personal belongings.

All my own older siblings from my mother lived here and those from my stepmother, too. The girls all slept in one room while the boys slept in the living room. By day the living room was neat but by nightfall all the mats were on the floor for us to sleep on. We did not have pillows or bedsheets and the mats were not porous. We covered ourselves with thin blankets that barely gave any warmth on the chilly floor. At night, some of the younger boys would wet the 'bed' and it smelled very bad. We would have to wash the mats during the day and hang them out on the clothesline to dry.

I attended kindergarten at Langata Nursery School for one year, then proceeded to Madaraka Primary School for Class One when I was six years old and was there eight years until Class Eight. Madaraka Primary School was within walking distance of our home. I have good memories of my primary school years. I enjoyed playing soccer during our recess, which was about twenty minutes long.

My siblings and I walked home for lunch as this was a cheaper option for my parents. With so many of us, they could not afford to have us carry little containers with packed lunches. Many times, we would eat whatever was left over from the previous night's supper, and that was not always enough to fill our little tummies. Many times, we went back to school for the afternoon classes quite hungry.

At home, we had no house help. Therefore, after school we each had chores to do. I learned to wash my clothes by hand and hang them out to dry on the clothesline. I cleaned the bathroom and toilet, which were in separate areas, and cooked for many people at a very young age. As I grew up, it felt like all these chores were punishment, but through them, I learned to appreciate the value of hard work. In retrospect, these chores helped to build my work ethic and character. By the time I got my own house as a young man, I had no problems keeping it clean and cooking for myself. As a married man, my wife was elated that I could cook some meals, and this gave her some free time away from the kitchen.

With my sisters Ruth and Betty in our home in Nairobi West

I remember that we always had some free time at home after doing our chores. During these times, when I was around eight to ten years old, I got to play with my siblings and other children in the neighborhood. We played soccer, hide and go seek, 'tapo' (tap someone and run), 'mkebe' (kick the can) and others. My favorites were soccer and rounders, which would get us all excited and competitive. Occasionally, we cheekily walked around the neighborhood and picked up lost coins on the ground. We would put these coins together until they were enough to get us a packet of chips (fries) from the nearby shops in Madaraka.

During holidays and school breaks I would go home to the village and spend time with my mom. On those days my mother would wake me up early to join her as she went to cultivate the farm. She assured me that we would be done by midday, so I did not complain too much. I often walked with her to the open-air market where people would go to sell their produce. We would take the bus partway and walk the rest of the way to save money. She taught me not to complain. She said that she would cook and watch me eat. It was her way of showing affection. In our culture, parents did not hug their children. My mother showed love and affection through cooking food for us.

Along with many good memories came some bad, and sometimes painful ones. A violation of my innocence by a couple of my siblings breaking sexual boundaries was difficult for me. It is unfortunate that nothing was done.

Also, some questions I had did not seem to have any answers. For example, I often wondered why my dad had to marry two wives. My father would tell me that I was as stupid as my mother and I felt deep pain upon hearing those words from him. Despite saying those hurtful words to me, he wanted me to become a doctor or to marry a nurse when I grew up. He anticipated that having a doctor or a nurse in the family would mean free medical consultation for him when he needed it. Medical fees in Kenya have always been extremely expensive for the common man.

When school trips were announced, I wanted to go on them but they were unaffordable. Although the fee was very minimal, my dad felt it was too much for him especially when he had to count the number of children that needed to go on these trips. I did not complain as I felt that it was better to use the money for buying food for the large household. There were so many of us and food was scarce. It was more important to have enough to eat. We cooked 'chapatis' and 'ugali' for supper, but beef was not in plentiful supply. Rice and beans were only cooked when Benta, my sister came home. My mother enjoyed cooking for visitors, removing maize from maize cobs and pounding millet to make flour.

As I got into my later primary years (around 12-14 years), I had to start getting serious with my education as I prepared to go to high school. At that time, our curriculum was dubbed '8-4-4' which was eight years of primary school, four years of high school and then four years of university.

In Class Eight, at the end of primary school, we had to write a country-wide examination called Kenya Certificate of Primary Education (KCPE). My first attempt at the KCPE exam did not turn out well. My grades did not satisfy the requirements to get me into the secondary school that I desired. As a result, I decided to repeat Class Eight. That was not a very easy decision, but I was determined to do better and get into a good secondary school. I was not alone. My brother, Omondi, also did not do very well and so we re-took Class Eight together. This time we changed schools from Madaraka Primary to Kalsi Primary School, which was not too far from home. I was not going to let what others thought about me deter me from my goal. I worked very hard that year and gave it my all. I recall doing so well that I got chosen to represent the school for city debates and quizzes against other schools. This boosted my self-esteem and confidence a great deal. Finally, the year came to an end and I sat the KCPE exam in 1986. I passed with much better grades that would get me into a good secondary school.

Secondary School

I was selected to go to Upper Hill Secondary School where I was to study for four years before going to university. My brother Omondi made it to the same school, too. Upper Hill Secondary was in those days a provincial 'Day School', meaning that students came and returned home after classes. Boarding schools had students who stayed on campus throughout the school term and returned home during school breaks.

I enjoyed my high school years and during this time I began to be a bit more social. I took a French class in Form One (first year of high school) and fell in love with the language. I took the class each year till I finished high school. I must admit that our French teacher made it so much easier to learn the language. Her name was Survana.

Unlike primary school where we had to go home for lunch, we were given lunch at school. I enjoyed this very much as we got some solid and healthy meals. My favorite day in school was Wednesday as we would eat French fries for lunch. On Thursdays we ate rice and beans, which I enjoyed as well. The portions were reasonable and filling.

As a student in Upper Hill Secondary School

One of my favorite subjects was math. Because I enjoyed it, I practiced it daily. It was my dad's favorite subject and I was sure that if I did well in it, he would be proud of me. I tried to work hard and get good grades to impress him. I recall one time when I got 99% in math and proudly went to show this to him. What I got in return pierced my heart. I was very discouraged by his response. He said, "Either you are the teacher's favorite, or the math is very easy."

Outside of school, I was involved in the Community Presbyterian Church (CPC) Madaraka—the church that I attended regularly. It was just about opposite our house. My brother Sila had introduced me and some of our family members to the church. I remember that I started attending CPC when I was in primary school and loved being in the Sunday School children's program. Some of the teachers who made an impact in my life were Keziah Ogutu and Loise Semenye. As a teenager I joined the Young People's Fellowship (YPF) with my good friends, (the late) Vincent Kisuvuli, Kamau Kanyi, Wilfred Amalemba, Malak Airo, Josephine and Martin Gatoto, Harrison Airo, and others. The most significant moment of my high school years came when I gave my life to Jesus Christ when I was about fifteen years old.

With a few of our CPC friends, now branded 'Warriors', gathered for our farewell in 2015

At the end of high school in Form Four, we sat a nationwide examination called Kenya Certificate of Secondary Education (KCSE). This exam—covering all the high school subjects—started in October and ran into November. I majored in physical sciences and focused on math, French, English and Swahili. I stayed away from the pure sciences as I was not very keen on a career in the sciences. The results of the KCSE examination would determine whether I gained entrance to the university. I sat for the exam in 1990.

In Upper Hill Secondary School uniform with brother Omondi

CHAPTER 3:

EARLY ADULTHOOD AND CAREER

Post-Secondary Education

The results of the KCSE exams came out in February of 1991. I was delighted to see my grade. I met the threshold for university entry! The next step was to find out which university I was selected to join. Within a short while I got the confirmation letter that I had been accepted at Kenyatta University to pursue a bachelor's degree in Education. My major was in French and English Literature. I was happy with this program choice as I had come to love the French language from the little I took of it in high school. Training to become a teacher was not my first choice. However, I accepted this and determined to do my best. My parents were happy that I got admission to university and accepted the program I had. They even liked the idea of my profession as a teacher.

We were to report to the university in 1991 but this was postponed until 1992. I was excited about this new season of my life, starting my road to independence away from home. I packed all my belongings into two bags for the 35-km journey from Karen, where I was living. To get to the university, I had to board two separate public transport vehicles. It took about an hour and a half to get to the campus. The registration process was simple, and I was assigned a room in the Nyandarua Hostel on the east side of the university. The shared room had two tiny beds separated by a wall for privacy. This was going to be my home for the duration of my four-year program.

In my hostel room at Kenyatta University

Kenyatta University was, by then, the second largest university in the country boasting of a student population of well over 10,000 students from all corners of the country. For many, this was their first time in the big city of Nairobi, since they had studied in rural areas all their lives. I felt glad that my father had insisted on us getting our education in the city. It gave me a very different outlook on life and I was able to settle down faster than those who came from upcountry.

Some of the highlights at the university were sharpening my knowledge of and fluency in the French language. The grammar part was a big challenge while conversation in French was not so hard for me. Outside of class, some of my classmates and I would constantly converse in French to the amazement of many other friends who were not in our class. These guys—Jason Mose, Davis Kamau, Deo Gumba, James Gichuru and I—helped each other gain confidence in speaking this language that was so foreign to us. Later in our careers, many of us used the French we learned.

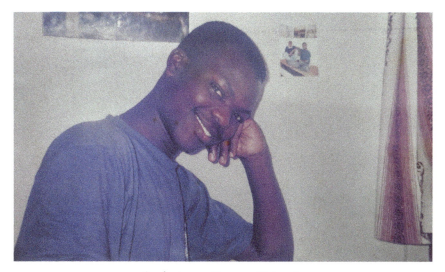

Study time at Kenyatta University

Another highlight was the social life I was able to have. I got involved in many activities on campus that boosted my self-image, self-confidence and social standing. Most of my siblings will testify that I was a very quiet boy at home, while my college mates, on the other hand, will attest to my outgoing, talkative nature.

As a Christian, I quickly got involved in the Christian programs on campus like Navigators and Christian Union Fellowship. I surrounded myself with friends from these groups and they helped to keep me accountable while cheering me on in my walk with God. It is from this same circle that I met my wonderful wife Christine.

*After a Christian Union fellowship at Kenyatta University
with Christine and my friend Davis*

Other friends from the fraternity whom I treasure to this day include Richard Mwikamba and Abel Mkombola. I also treasure my good roommates, David Osedo and Tom Kiuna, who made staying in the hostels so much more fun. David was like a brother who kept me focused when I seemed to get distracted. He loved God and encouraged me to hold on to Him always. He challenged me to work hard in university and life.

Another highlight was being a peer counselor under the Family Life Education program offered by the Students' Association on campus. It was sponsored by Pathfinder International. Together with other student peer counselors, we received a lot of training in Family Life and Reproductive Health that equipped us to be knowledgeable and effective in serving our student community in this area. Serving as a peer counselor built my confidence and competence in one-on-one interactions and group facilitation.

My four years of university finally came to an end in 1996. I graduated with a bachelor's degree in Education with a Major in French and English Literature. Our graduation was held in October of the same year. It was a joyous occasion for me and my extended family who came from all over to celebrate with me. Christine, whom I was dating by this time, also graduated that same year.

Graduation day at Kenyatta University with Christine, October 1996

In 2002, I decided to start a master's program at the University of Nairobi. I enrolled in the Master of Business Administration program as a part-time student. Because I was now working full-time and raising a family simultaneously, this meant it would take longer than two years to complete the program. I chose to major in marketing because I enjoyed talking to people and was quite confident in my sales skills. I had discovered that I could easily connect with and identify the needs of a group of people.

University of Nairobi is the largest university in Kenya and being a student there was considered prestigious. If you said that you were a graduate of the University of Nairobi, you gained respect that was distinct from other local universities. Doing my master's degree gave me a lot of prestige. However, it was tough completing my MBA. Since I did not have any accounting background, I struggled with Financial Accounting and Managerial Accounting. Luckily, I had a relative, Duncan Oduor, who was an expert in accounting. He offered to give me some free tutorials which helped me a great deal in mastering the concepts. I am truly thankful for his kind heart in supporting me in that way. Because of him, Marketing Units, together with Research Methods, were much easier for me.

For my final, I wrote one of the most unique marketing theses in the university titled "The Impact of Sex Appeal in Motor Vehicle Purchase Intention". I thoroughly enjoyed doing this project even though it took everything I had to research and write it.

In Marketing, I loved the areas of Brand Management and Consumer Behavior best. I will always remember Ms. Margaret Ombok, Mr. Ogutu and Mrs. Ngoje as some of the professors that inspired and encouraged me the most.

I also found it challenging making the commute to the university, which was close to the city center while my office was way out in Embakasi about 15 km away. Having to navigate the rush-hour traffic on Mombasa Road was an arduous task and it would take me about one and a half hours to get to class. Classes would typically start at 6 pm and run up to about 9-10 pm during the week, and then I would make my way home to my family. Since I could only afford to take two to three units per semester, it took me close to five years to finish this program. I finally graduated in 2006 and this was a very big achievement for me.

During my MBA graduation

Work Life and Career

Work for me began when I completed high school. I moved out of the family home in Nairobi West and went to live with my eldest brother Raphael, who by then had his own home in Karen. He had a radio studio at the Wilson Airport where I started working, doing odd jobs like painting the walls during their renovation. When he finally built an office in Karen, there was more work needed in painting, setting up office furniture and producing videos. After I started university, I was not able to work there much except when I was on break in between semesters. Raphael gave me a foundation by allowing me to work in his company at an early age, which created a stronger work ethic in me while preparing me for the job market. I am glad I had a strong brother. He showed me how to survive by being tough on me yet allowing me to learn from my mistakes. He modeled entrepreneurship by working hard and working smart.

After I completed my Bachelor of Education degree, I was called to work for the Teachers Service Commission (TSC), which was the umbrella employer for teachers in the public schools in the country. This meant that they had the power to send teachers to work in any school across the country where they were needed. I was curious to find out where they would send me. I was utterly shocked and dismayed to find out that I had been posted to a very remote high school in the rural western part of Kenya. I was to be a French teacher there. After much thought and processing, I decided against taking up the offer as I did not want to live in such a remote area where my career aspirations would not be further developed. TSC would not consider my wish to be posted somewhere else, so I lost that opportunity for employment.

As I pondered and prayed about what next, Raphael employed me formally to work for his communications company in 1997. I started off as a Customer Service Executive where I handled specific client accounts. As a further incentive, I was offered extra pay on commission for any new business I brought in. I was excited about this opportunity and decided to give it my all. This was also about the time I became engaged to Christine and we were preparing for our wedding. I was determined to work hard and get enough to get us started on a new life together.

At my first job at ACE Communications

As young adults we did not have our own car. We used public transportation called 'matatu', which is a small minivan to seat about 12-15 passengers. We also used the public buses that were then run by Kenya Bus Services. These public transportation vehicles were reliable but travel took a lot of time. My first goal was to buy my own car to enable me to get around much easier, especially for personal errands, which I could not do with the company vehicles. I recall my first sale towards the end of 1997. I got a fat commission that was enough to help me purchase my first car—a Nissan Salon. It was exciting to own a car. I took Christine out much more frequently and we did all the errands for our wedding.

Hanging out with Christine during my lunch at Kenyatta International Conference Centre KICC

I worked at ACE Communications Ltd. until 2000, when I felt I wanted to get some experience away from the family business. I managed to get a job with a clearing and logistics company called SDV Transami (Group Bollore) based in Embakasi area. I worked as a Client Service Executive where I was given my own set of clients to serve. After about a year, I was seconded to sit at one of the major client's premises, Unilever Kenya, as their Account Executive. I felt honored to be based there and I was treated like one of their own employees in many ways. I enjoyed some of the same privileges as the staff who worked there. I got to meet a wide range of employees who became friends, not just to me but to my wife as well.

I resigned from this job in 2005 to complete my MBA in order to add value to Floral Interiors, which was the business Christine was running full-time. Together Christine and I developed a business plan that aimed to diversify and grow the business. Initially we focused on retailing fresh flowers for weddings, corporate clients and individuals. Our long-range plan was to incorporate Landscaping and Interior Décor all under one banner, Floral Interiors Ltd.

I began the landscaping component by personally taking it upon myself reclaim a deserted community playground in our neighborhood and turning into a beautiful space that all could enjoy. I knew that for anyone to have confidence in our work, they needed to see something visually appealing. This piece of land was overgrown with bushes and weeds, making it not just an eyesore but too dangerous for our children to play on. I organized labor to clear and clean up the mess. Then we began to prepare the ground for healthy grass, flowers and hedges. Soon it became a beautiful area for kids to play, adults to take walks and families to gather in for small parties. This project captured the attention of the City Council, who were impressed and offered to install lighting that made the place more secure at night.

One of our landscaping projects

We now felt more confident to advertise for landscaping business. We offered several proposals and were blessed to get our first major contract in the year 2011 with one of the prestigious corporate organizations in Embakasi area. I used my networks and other forums to market our services and products. This business sustained us for the period I was not in full-time employment and still in school.

My brother Raphael mentioned that he was tired of running the communication company and he wanted to dispose of it. I expressed my interest to take it over and run it now that I had more time on my hands. I had worked there long enough to know that the business had great potential, so I ambitiously stepped out in faith. I put in a lot of resources to try and get it back on its feet, including taking up a very big office space to attract large corporate clients. Unfortunately, many people had come into the industry, working right from their homes using very simple technology. We could not compete on the same level and thus the business did not take off as I had hoped. However, the experience was worth the risk.

Work trip to Mexico in 2010

In 2014, I decided to go back into employment with my brother again. This time I worked at his new establishment, a posh restaurant in the plush Karen suburb. I was their marketing consultant, handling most of the clients' customer experience and sales. I loved interacting with the staff and guests and felt a great sense of satisfaction when clients were happy with our service. Since this job came at the peak of our plans to relocate to Canada for studies, I was forced to give it up when we got our visas to travel together as a family in June of 2015.

Moving to Canada meant a new shift in my career. I was not sure what to expect in terms of the kind of work I would get. Many people in Kenya looked down on some of the jobs in the west, especially the manual type of jobs. They did not think much of jobs in the fast food or supermarket industry, either. Generally blue-collar jobs in Kenya are thought to be for those who have not had much education and are poorly remunerated. In the west, however, such jobs are well remunerated and require some level of skill. Since I was granted an open work permit, I could work in any industry that I wished as long as it was legitimate.

After getting Christine and the boys settled in college and school respectively, I started to focus on looking for work. I had been psychologically prepared before coming here that I might not get my dream job right away. Therefore, I was ready to start anywhere that was entry level with my skills. I purposed to enjoy the journey of work. My first job was a manual one offered by a friend called Marvin. I was to paint the walls of his mum's house. I felt confident I could do this as I had done some painting previously back home in Kenya for our house and office. I was so proud of myself and could hardly put down the clean waterproof Canadian bills I was paid. I got to interact with Marvin's mum (now deceased) quite a lot and felt a sense of belonging as she said she would now be my Canadian mother.

I remember attending a job exhibition at Medicine Hat College. I got to meet potential employers and I landed a job at a fast-food restaurant. Having worked for a restaurant back in Kenya gave me an advantage. They were impressed with my skills and experience and decided to train me for management.

I was excited about this opportunity and started by working in the back office to gain supervision experience. That involved doing the manual tasks at both the front and back end of the restaurant just like the rest of the crew.

I was given shift work, which meant that my work days and hours would vary from week to week. Some weeks I worked twenty-five hours in total while other weeks I worked much less. I learned to be very flexible and adaptive, especially with some of the tasks I was not used to doing as a manager back home. The fact that I was being trained for management motivated me to stay on. Unfortunately, there was no timeline as to when this would happen—if at all.

Meanwhile, a dear lady from church who heard about my teaching experience asked if I would be interested in working in the schools. She referred me to a key contact at one of the local school boards to find out if there were any teaching opportunities. I sent in my resume and shortly after, I was called for an interview. Since this was going to be a regular day job, I reduced my hours at the fast food restaurant. I took evening shifts so that I could work at the school during the day. After some time, I realized I was not young and fit enough to work a night and day job, so I resigned from the restaurant. I focused only on the day job at the elementary school

My education degree gave me the confidence to work in a learning environment both at Elm Street and George Davison Schools. I met some of the warmest people in my life and extend my gratitude to Reagan Weeks, Joely Augustino, Nikki Johansen, Emma Piayda, Natalie Oliphant, Mario, Tara Lee, Tricia Unreiner, and Richelle Thomas.

Ski trip with school some the school kids in Canada

Our principal at Elm Street was a very special lady called Reagan Weeks. She was an outgoing person yet very firm in how she dealt with most of the kids who had serious behavior issues. She saw the potential in me and challenged me to go higher. She, as a marketer too, encouraged me to seek out some part-time work at Medicine Hat College as an instructor in the Business Department. She had worked there in the past and knew some people whom I could talk to for more information. I was pleasantly surprised when another friend from church told me about an opportunity at the college as a part-time instructor in the Business Department.

I was excited about this as I felt that my master's degree in Business Administration was finally going to be put to use. I put in my application and was elated to be given one of the three positions as a Part-Time Instructor of Marketing, which was my major. This position was teaching an evening class for only one semester and fit well with my day job at the school. I took the job and taught the evening class at the college. I was grateful that I could be of value in this way. It was a very enriching and enlightening experience.

This part-time position came to an end in April 2016 and I continued with my day job in School District 76. I started with one year at Elm Street School and then went to the George Davison Elementary School, where I have been until my illness forced me to go on medical leave. I cherish all the teaching staff and students at both schools.

For me, the highlight was teaching English as a Second Language at George Davison School. English comes naturally to me and teaching children of many nationalities gave me a deep sense of satisfaction as I watched their comprehension and fluency expand.

Classes typically ended at 3 pm and I did not need to stay around the school. This allowed me enough time to spend with my family. This work schedule helped me balance my work and life in a way that saw my own children grow well in their schoolwork, extracurricular activities and family time.

My mother-in-law visited me at work in Medicine Hat in June 2017

CHAPTER 4:

COURTSHIP AND MARRIAGE

It all began in 1992 when I was a first-year student at Kenyatta University. As a young Christian, while attending a weekly *Navigators Kenya* meeting, Loyce Christine Wangui Igeria arrived a few minutes late in a long blue flowered dress. Believe me, it was hard not to be distracted by her. I remember the day just like it was yesterday. We introduced ourselves as 'freshers' (first-year students) and Christine just stood out for me. From that day on we became casual friends and as we grew in our relationship over the years, we discovered we had many common interests. For one thing, we were both born-again Christians who had given our lives to Jesus Christ while in high school. At the university, we both attended the Navigators fellowship and Christian Union.

Another common thread was that we were both artists. I loved portrait drawing while she studied a more hands-on kind of art. She was taking a Bachelor of Arts degree in Fine Art. I often joined her as she burnt the midnight oil meeting her art project deadlines. I am not a night owl, but I managed to stay awake in her company. I lived on the east side of the campus in a hostel known as Nyandarua, but Christine lived on the west side. A twenty-minute stroll to her hostel did not bother me nor did it seem distant at the time. On several occasions I helped carry her art material across the campus to her hostel or back to the studios. It must have been true love in the making.

During our semester-long breaks, the university students were expected to vacate the university rooms and return to our respective homes. We were expected to take all our belongings with us. At times, we got lucky enough to borrow a car from a relative, and not have to use public transportation. I lived with my older brother Raphael in the Karen area. Christine lived with her mom and siblings in the Parklands area, about forty minutes from where I lived. During the campus breaks, we did not get to see each other much but we did talk on phone. These were precious minutes because we did not have cell phones. We did not have much alone time for private talk. I used to work at my older brother's office during my breaks and I did not get much free time to see Christine. Occasionally, I would dash over to her house and say a quick "hi" if I was driving in the neighborhood.

In our third year of university, we both became peer counselors on campus under a student program sponsored by Pathfinders International and organized by the University Students' Association. As peer counselors, we conducted lots of activities on campus for fellow students. Some of the activities included peer talks, video shows and one-on-one sessions. This service to our college community brought Christine and I much closer together. We were able to meet and interact with a wide range of the student population.

It was also during this time that I began having intimate feelings for Christine. This was quite tricky for me because I knew she was dating someone else. Luckily for me, this guy was in a different university, and he was not able to see her as often as I was. We were such good friends that we were both completely open about our relationships. I had a few brushes with girls on campus, but none ever became serious. I did not want to push Christine into anything serious yet if she was not ready. I believed in the saying, "If you love the bird, set it free; if it is meant for you, it will stay." I was confident that if it was meant to be, then she would be mine.

It was not too long before she admitted to me that the relationship with the other guy had broken up. I wasn't sure if I was to be sad for her, but secretly, I was glad that it was working for me. I decided to be there for her, a shoulder for her to lean on, and slowly, I 'won' her over. I confess it did feel good. I felt I had conquered the world.

We started dating seriously in 1995. By the time we were in our fourth year in university, we were madly in love. Our plans for life after university coincided since we both wanted to work and live in Nairobi. We both had ideas about marriage; after all we had gotten into this relationship with that in mind. Being in our mid-twenties, we did not have time to play around and wanted to settle down as soon as possible. All we needed was to get stable jobs, enabling us to get a house and stay together.

Dating in 1997

By this time, I was visiting Christine more frequently at home during breaks, and on weekends off campus. Christine introduced me to some of her family members and most of them were welcoming and friendly to me. They did not show any discrimination to me despite my being from a different ethnic community. I am from the Luo community while Christine is from the Kikuyu. For many years, these two communities had been political rivals and it was not easy to get family support for intercultural marriage.

Being Christians made a big difference for us. We saw ourselves first as children of God and not members of an ethnic community. We were determined to both honor our parents and also do what was best for each other. We were not going to let our different backgrounds come between us.

Growing up, my parents had their own reservations about marrying someone from the Kikuyu community. I was concerned about how they would receive Christine. My mom did not want me to marry a Kikuyu girl because she worried the girl would go away with my kids if we divorced. My dad felt the same as my mom and wanted me to marry a Luo, a nurse or doctor. However, my mom also wanted me to marry whomever I loved and said that they both would help me love her.

Mom lived upcountry in Asembo, about 400 km from Nairobi. Because of the distance and high travel costs, I did not get to see her frequently. Finally, the day came to introduce Christine to my mother. A family event was held in Nairobi. It provided the perfect opportunity for the introduction.

My mom fell in love with Christine the moment she met her. I was pleasantly surprised when she greeted Christine warmly. Later she told me that she liked her. This blew me away and confirmed that God was in this relationship.

My other siblings and family members living in Nairobi had already met her and had given me a 'thumbs up', too. This meant a lot to me because, in Kenya, marriage involves more than only the couple's desires. It is a large family affair. Having good relationships on both sides was one step to reducing unnecessary conflict with in-laws.

I formally proposed to Christine towards the end of 1997. I bought her a beautiful engagement ring from a jewelry store in downtown Nairobi. She cherished that ring like gold. It was the seal of my commitment to our relationship and our future. We set December 5th, 1998, as our wedding date, which gave us ample time to prepare financially and plan the necessary pre-wedding events.

Courtship; attending an evening cocktail with Christine

Before the actual wedding day there were three essential meetings to be held: two main meetings and one final meeting between our two families. The most important event was the first meeting between the two families. I was expected to officially declare my intentions for marriage. Since we were from different communities and cultures, we each had distinct marriage ceremony practices. We chose a middle ground that inclined more to Christine's family customs.

Traditionally, most Kenyan families ask for a bride price from the groom's family. This is almost always terrifying to young men who want to marry because it tends to be a very expensive affair that most cannot afford. I was fortunate that Christine's family spared me this trauma. As a Christian family, they did not ask for a bride price because they believed that a child can never really be 'paid for'. With that in mind, her family simply asked me to give whatever token of appreciation I could give. This was done during the second meeting held at Christine's home.

The last ceremony, according to the Kikuyu tradition, was to visit the home of the young man to see where the daughter would be moving. Since my home meant where my parents lived, this was going to be upcountry in my Asembo village. Unfortunately, time was not on our side to make this visit before the wedding. We did, however, reach an agreement to visit after the wedding. We honored this agreement a few months after our wedding.

At one of the Kikuyu ceremonies before the wedding at Christine's home

Along with these family meetings, we chose to prepare for marriage as a couple by attending premarital counseling sessions. We were connected to a special couple, David and Jane Mutiga. They willingly agreed to mentor us in preparation for our marriage. We attended weekly sessions in their home, talking about various aspects of marriage. We observed how they interacted with each other and with their two children. They modeled our ideal Christian marriage and parenting. We admired them and aspired to be like them. The Mutiga's stood by and prayed with us both before and after our wedding. In addition, we had some counseling sessions with Pastor Gregory Kivanguli, who was then based at Nairobi Pentecostal Church where Christine was a member. He was also the presiding minister at our wedding. He shared God's perspective of a Christian marriage. He was very real and practical in his sessions. This provided a strong foundation for our marriage.

On a personal level, we also took time to study a book on marriage. We chose a study guide titled "Before You Say I Do" that took an in-depth look at topics such as finances, roles and responsibilities, children, intimacy and in-laws. We talked about each of these topics, decided how we wanted our marriage to be and planned a unified foundation for our marriage. We also had time to pray and commit all these issues to God as we prepared for this lifelong journey. Some important things we committed to were to start and maintain a joint bank account and budget our finances as one. We also planned for two children after about 1-2 years of marriage. As well, we decided that we were not going to live apart from each other even for work commitments for more than six months. That's why, when we planned to come to Canada for Christine's study, we decided to travel together as a family and not be separated by Christine going alone.

I must admit that despite some of these plans, I did make some mistakes along the way. Once or twice I went behind Christine's back and bought expensive 'gadgets' using the family income without her knowledge. When she finally got to know about these incidents, it was not good for me. We ended up with some serious conflicts before we got it all resolved.

Throughout this process, I got to know and see the deeper side of Christine. I saw a truly beautiful, gentle, loving and caring person. Over the years, I have come to know Christine as a hardworking, sensitive and deeply committed friend. She helped me focus not just on the wedding day, but on what was more important—our marriage.

We had set up a wedding committee to help plan and organize the wedding. This committee was composed of faithful friends from my Community Presbyterian Church led by George Ogutu as the Chairman and some of Christine's friends. Friends contributed in various ways to help meet the wedding budget. I was the only one working because Christine's new job did not start until after the wedding. It was a big miracle as our finances were limited. We saw God provide and meet every need, including for our honeymoon.

My goal was to move out of Raphael's house in Karen just before the wedding so that we could start preparing our place for life together after the wedding. Christine and I found a small suite in the South C area and the rent was affordable with only one income. It extended from the main house and had a small living room, kitchenette and bathroom. It was sweet and just enough for the two of us when we get married. I moved in a month before the wedding and Christine moved in after our honeymoon.

The wedding day finally came on December 5th, 1998. It was a nice cool Saturday. The ladies from my church, my aunt and my mom accompanied my best man Vincent Matisha (late) pick Christine up at her home in the Upper Hill area. He was to ensure she made it to church on time. The service was to begin at 10 am. I remember waiting anxiously at the front for her to arrive. I had not slept much the night before in anticipation of the big day. She arrived on time and the ceremony went smoothly. It was a special occasion crafted in heaven. This was not a covenant to be taken lightly. As I write this, I recall our wedding vows, now accentuated with more meaning than they had twenty years ago. I never thought that the reality of *"in sickness and health"* would be so grueling. Christine has been by my side throughout my diagnosis and illness with such a deep love and loyalty.

Our wedding day, December 5, 1998, at Nairobi Pentecostal Church

Our wedding day, with our parents, brother Arthur Igeria and page boy Mburu Igeria

After the wedding service, we took wedding pictures in the beautiful gardens at The Fairview Hotel. This was a special time for the bridal party to bond and refresh after a tense one-hour service on our feet. I recall our little page boy Mburu Igeria, at only three years old, holding tightly onto Christine. He was her first nephew and they had spent many special times together. Our maid of honor, Wangari Muriithi, tried to keep him occupied and assured him that his aunt was in good hands with Uncle Kefa, her new love.

After pictures and refreshments, we all found our way to the reception grounds. As a bridal party, we drove together, in the beautifully decorated bridal limousine. The rest of the bridal party followed slowly in separate vehicles decorated with ribbons and bows, all coordinated in our wedding colors. The reception venue was the University of Nairobi Chiromo Campus grounds. It was beautifully decorated with bright flowers, balloons and fabric—all color-coordinated. The tents were stark white and covered us all from the elements. So many relatives and friends attended. We were so overwhelmed by the love and gifts showered on us that day.

Our wedding reception, sharing cake

Since then we have had the continual support of friends and family helping us to weather the storms and enjoy the blessings. On December 5th, 2018, we celebrated twenty years of marriage.

One group that helped us was the 'NDOA' (marriage) Group, which was composed of Kate and Edwin Tongoi, Mary and George Otieno, Adrine and Anthony Thuku, and Catherine and Paul Kimotho. As a group, we began to meet once a month in one of our homes. We would share a meal, laugh and talk about specific aspects of marriage, including some of our challenges as couples. These sessions not only solidified our marriages but provided support networks. As children came along, they were not left behind. They accompanied us to the meetings and found good friendships in each other, too, while their parents met in a separate room. We continued to meet faithfully for several years until life's transitions made it difficult for us to meet physically. Paul and Catherine relocated to Tanzania, then Christine and I moved to Canada, and lastly Kate and Edwin moved to Australia. However, we continue to talk, encourage and pray for one another on a social media group chat called WhatsApp.

As a couple, we have tried our best to do lots of activities together to bring us closer together. We attend social groups together and this helps us connect well with others. I find it easier to make friends in groups and enjoy meeting new people. We try to make friends as a couple as much as possible. This way we have had a wider group of family friends while still giving each other time and space to have individual friends. My friends became Christine's friends and vice versa.

Before we were married, Christine and I attended different churches. After the wedding, we decided to attend my church together, the Community Presbyterian Church in Madaraka. Christine had been attending the Nairobi Pentecostal Church on Valley Road. She was adaptable and settled well into CPC even though it was very different from what she was used to. We served in Sunday School Ministry together and attended a common Bible Study group once a week.

Hiking in Kajiado, Kenya, 2011

Hiking at Kitmikayi Rocks, Nyanza, Kenya, 2014

After Matthew was born, we felt prompted to move to another church. After much prayer, we settled for Mavuno Church, which was interdenominational. It was a vibrant church with a largely younger age demographic. At one point we were viewed as the older crop that the younger ones looked up to. It was easier to get into leadership positions and we felt we had much to offer the younger generation. We joined the Marriage Ministry dubbed "NDOA" and started off as facilitators, taking younger couples through a ten-week class for marriage preparation.

Later we joined the parenting ministry dubbed "LEA", also as facilitators, and sometimes did some administrative work to keep the classes running smoothly for ten weeks in a row. We met and served with many amazing people. As the bonds grew, we began to meet with some of them on a monthly basis to encourage ourselves in the journey of parenting. It was very fulfilling and an honor to serve God in this way as we knew we were in no way perfect or qualified to do so. However, we knew that God looks at the heart and works through those who depend on Him. We are so humbled by the many lives that we were able to impact through this service.

One of our bonding gatherings with LEA facilitators in Nairobi, Kenya

Among other things, my greatest pleasures as an adult have been with my wife and going out for dinner together. My mom's best way to express love was by cooking. So, to me it seemed that the best way to show love to my wife was through food. Rarely did I give her gifts like flowers (maybe I should have because food was not be her love language).

One of my biggest challenge during young adulthood was finances. We needed life insurance but rent consumed most of our money. However, we tried to educate ourselves on good money management and tried to keep our expenses in check so that we had enough to see us through each month. I believe we have been able to live a modest life for the most part. Trusting in God as our provider made it easier to handle our finances, too. Tithing was an integral part of our budget and we never lacked as God continued to meet our needs.

Attending a social event with Christine

Featured in Kenyan 'Parents' magazine in August 2015

Featured in Kenyan 'Parents' magazine in August 2015

Moving to Canada was an opportunity for adventure, not just as a couple, but as a family. We enjoyed the experience of starting all over again in a new country, house and job hunting, meeting new people, serving in a new church and raising our boys here. One thing I love about Canada so far are the parks, which are clean, safe and well maintained. I enjoyed taking walks with Christine in the parks and sitting quietly for personal retreats. During our retreats, we took time to reflect on our lives, where we were at and where we hoped to go. We talked about our boys and what we desired to see in their lives. We also spent time praying and committing ourselves to God. We knew that we needed God's grace to see us through all the challenges that life brought our way. We had a lot to be grateful for as well and we made time to write down all these in thanksgiving to God.

Arrival at Calgary International Airport, Canada, August 17th, 2015

Our 20th wedding anniversary arrived on December 5th, 2018, just as I was finishing this memoir. I was grateful to be alive to see this milestone in our lives. A friend of mine helped me get Christine some lovely flowers and a card. Christine, on the other hand, surprised me with a wedding band, a replacement for my wedding band that was stolen at gun point several years ago while in Kenya. Along with our boys, we were able to go out and enjoy a hearty meal at one of our favorite restaurants in town. The journey of marriage continues to be one that is tried and tested in many ways. I have grown through the many ups and downs, falling and rising up again. I am glad that I do have God on my side to help us walk this road.

See Chapter 9 for the story of how I lost my ring.

CHAPTER 5:

CHILDREN

Children are a blessing from the Lord. It was indeed a great joy when we found out that Christine was expecting our first child at the beginning of the year 2000. We were so overjoyed that we decided not to find out the sex of the baby, but rather wait for the surprise at birth. This put us in a tight spot when it came to shopping and preparing for the baby. We decided to get neutral-colored clothing for the first few weeks and then shop later after baby came.

As for naming, we had to pick out both girls' and boys' names, just in case. If it was a girl, we were going to name her 'Serena', mainly because we just loved the name and it was going to signify the serene and tranquil girl we were going to have. If it was a boy, we were going to name him 'Jonathan', a Biblical name meaning "God has given." These were going to be their first names. We still had to decide on the second/middle names for each.

Traditionally, naming is taken very seriously, and every community has their way of giving names to each child. In my community (Luo), a child is named depending on the time of day that they are born, be it a girl or a boy. These names are specific to the time of day—early morning, mid-morning, afternoon, evening and late night. In Christine's community, children are named after grandparents, aunts or uncles. The first son is named after the paternal grandfather and the first daughter is named after the paternal grandmother. The second son is named after the maternal grandfather whereas the second daughter is named after the maternal grandmother. We came to an agreement to pick out what would work for us and find a balance. To some extent, this meant departing from the traditional way of naming.

Jonathan, our first child, was born early Sunday morning on September 17th, 2000, at about 1:45 am. We chose Igeria as his middle name. This was in honor of Christine's late father, who died when she was only two years old.

Welcoming baby Jonathan home, September 2000

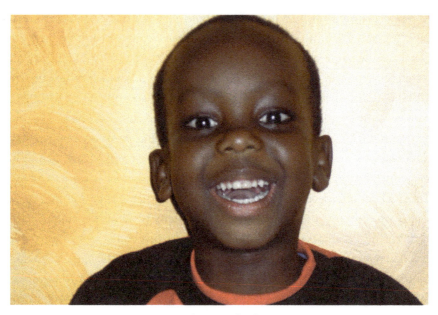

Jonathan, our firstborn

For our next child, we again wanted the excitement of not knowing the sex of the baby in advance. I thought it was going to be a girl, while Christine felt strongly that she was carrying another boy. She went into labor on Thursday, September 16th, 2004, during the day, but it was not until early evening that we raced to Emergency room. This was my second time to witness the labor and delivery of our child. The first was a bit traumatic but this second time, I felt much more confident. I rubbed her back and cheered her on, together with her sister Sally Gitonga, who rushed to be with us during this special moment. We all hoped that baby would be born on the 17th as this was Jonathan's birthday. However, we could not hold it back and baby was delivered after three hours of intense labor. Another boy!

Matthew, our second-born

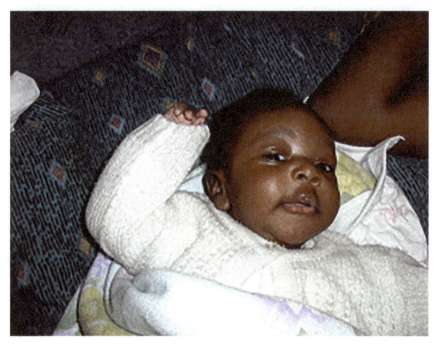

Matthew as a baby in October 2004

We had a name ready, Matthew, a Biblical name meaning "gift of the Lord." His middle name was to be Tuju in honor of my paternal grandfather, whom I never had the privilege of meeting. Raising these two boys has been a joy, an honor and a great privilege from God. Each one is unique and special in his own way.

From an early age, Jonathan has been outgoing, friendly and jovial. He confidently greeted neighbors walking by the house even before they approached him. He was easygoing and did not have any reservations when handled by a new babysitter. He began play school early at about two years and this helped to build his social skills. He continues to be a loyal friend and is very sensitive to the needs of others.

Matthew, on the other hand, has a quieter, more reserved personality. From an early age, he has exhibited a caring spirit, aware of the less privileged or those with special needs around him and wanting to help meet their needs. He is a go-getter and will not stop or give up until he gets what he wants. This came out strongly in his zeal for sports and wanting to be at his best in each game he played.

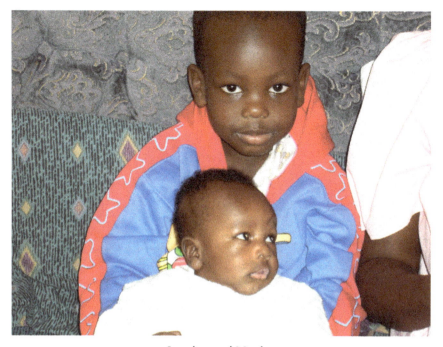

Jonathan and Matthew

Before our children were born, Christine and I took a parenting course to equip us to raise Godly children. We prayed for wisdom and guidance in parenting with a goal of raising a Godly generation. We were guided by the Bible verse in Proverbs 22:6, "Train up a child in the way he should go, and when he is old, he will not depart from it." We began by dedicating our boys to the Lord. We committed to taking them to church faithfully and teaching them the Word of God at home as well as in school. We engaged them in Christian activities that would connect them with other children, build Christian character and have fun in a healthy way. Some of these activities included Sunday School, youth programs, Christian camps and Bible Quizzing.

The boys and I attending a wedding

From the start, Christine and I planned to give our boys the best in extracurricular activities alongside their main schooling to build on their God-given talents and abilities. At different times of their lives, we enrolled them in activities such as swimming, piano, guitar, drums, skating, basketball, volleyball, soccer, football, rugby and drama. As they grew older, they focused their choices on activities using their strongest abilities, interests and time. I must admit that these activities were very demanding financially and time-wise. At times, Christine and I would have to separately take each child to their respective activities since they often occurred at the same time but in different locations. Yet it also has been rewarding to see the boys grow in their specific areas of interest. Each of their rooms is now adorned with medals and certificates to show their achievements along the way. They continue to learn the importance of being part of a team and the rewards of personal effort in individual undertakings.

Matthew started soccer as a little four-year-old boy

The boys skating

Music recital; Matthew on drums, Jonathan on bass guitar with teacher

Education has always been a priority for us. I did not want to impose on my children what they should be in life. Rather I have always wanted to give them the best opportunity to succeed in their individual dreams and aspirations. I always made it a point to attend school meetings and conferences with their teachers to assess their progress. As a trained teacher, I found it much easier to help them with their homework and found fulfillment when they mastered new concepts.

A time came when the schools they attended changed locations and were a great distance from where we lived. There was no bussing system. Every day we had to drive across the city to get them to the new location. With the traffic jams in Nairobi City, it became increasingly difficult to get them to school on time and then go to work, so we opted to pull them out and homeschool them. This happened during the whole school year of 2014-2015. We were lucky enough to be in a school system that could also be implemented at home. It was a Christian American-designed curriculum. This helped to make their transition to Canadian school a little easier the following year when we relocated as a family.

Our boys off to primary school, January 2009

The homeschooling experience drew me closer to the boys in many ways. I felt more in control of their learning. Christine and I became a good team in running our small learning center called "Dunamis School." It was one of the most enriching and fulfilling years of my life. We were not able to continue homeschooling the boys when we relocated to Canada and they were enrolled in the mainstream school system while I went to work.

As I write this memoir, Jonathan is in Grade 12, set to graduate in June 2019, and Matthew is in Grade 9. Jonathan hopes to build a career in IT while Matthew wants to pursue marketing like his dad. I am very keen to see what they will choose as career paths eventually.

The boys as teens; my pride and joy, July 2018

Raising the boys has not always been a bed of roses. We have had our fair share of challenges. One frightening time was when Matthew was about nine months old. He had a mysterious bout of high fevers that lasted for over a month. He was admitted to a children's hospital in Nairobi for treatment. We were so terrified when we were told he would need a bone marrow transfusion. At another point, a different pediatrician was convinced that he had tuberculosis and started him on very strong TB medication, which began to stunt his growth. After several tests, a faulty diagnosis and a second opinion that he had a viral infection, he was discharged to come home. It was on one of these days that one of our good friends visited and we laid hands on him in prayer. We cried out to God for his healing and from that day, the fevers left, and Matthew has been fine ever since. His growth continues to be on point.

The teen years really put a strain on our relationship with each other and the boys. No one can ever prepare you for the changes that come with teenage years: raging hormones, peer pressure, along with body and brain changes. I have learned to be flexible and very understanding to manage this period without losing them. My relationship with God has helped me extend grace and love to the boys.

As I ponder life and think about what really matters, I realize that a relationship with my children is what they will remember as they transition into their own adult lives. A relationship not just with me but with their Heavenly Father is the best legacy I can leave to them. In the meantime, I pray that my life will be an example for them to emulate. Right now, something tells me 'instinctively' to focus on a Godly legacy for my children.

My Certificate of Recognition

Matthew in Medicine Hat with gold medal

Jonathan with his soccer medal in Medicine Hat

CHAPTER 6:

THE MOVE

In 2006 a friend introduced Christine and I to the idea of moving to Canada. We were so thrilled about it and the opportunities that life in Canada presented. We quickly began to look at the requirements of immigration as skilled workers. I was in the process of completing my master's degree while Christine was already managing her floral business. We believed we had what it took to qualify to be accepted.

We sought some legal services and began to sell some of our belongings in preparation for this move. It was going to cost us quite a large amount of money. It was clear that the processing times for the applications were 36 months. Each month we waited with bated breath for ours to come through. Unfortunately, after 36 months, we had not heard anything from the immigration department. Within that time so much had happened in our lives that we decided to withdraw our application. We convinced ourselves that the move was probably never meant to be, and we continued with our lives and careers in Kenya.

As years went by, my younger brother Ngala moved to Canada as a student. He began to encourage us to think again about making the move. After our first attempt, we had cold feet and we dismissed all his efforts to make us reconsider.

However, in the year 2014, Christine began to feel the need for a change in her career. She was now ready to make the bold move to go back to school and was willing this time to go out of the country. Our sister-in-law Judy (Ngala's wife) happened to be visiting Kenya from Canada. She heard about

Christine's plans to go back to school and suggested considering Canada because moving there with the family would be easier than going to some other countries. Our interest grew again, but this time with more caution. We wanted to manage our own expectations therefore we did not put too much energy into it. We prayed about it and asked God to make it very clear to us this time as we did not want to waste any resources that did not need to go into this project. Everything had become more expensive during the eight years since our first attempt.

Sure enough, God began to make it clearer day by day. Christine managed to get all our paperwork organized promptly and got admitted into a college. God began to provide all that we needed miraculously, and we did not have to sell any of our possessions beforehand. With these doors opening, we began to invest a bit more of our emotional energy into the move.

We took time to go out as a family and talk about what moving to Canada would mean for all four of us. I recall sitting at the café at Nakumatt Mega Supermarket where we listed all the pros and cons of the move. This helped us make a better-informed decision.

Some of our friends were opposed to the idea and tried to dissuade us. However, there were others who were very supportive and felt God leading them to encourage us to keep exploring. We had to look at all that was presented to us and bring that before God for wisdom and guidance as to His perfect plan for us. We were not going to risk going into this major decision on our own. We did not want to do anything that was out of God's will for our lives. We continued to sense His leading and direction towards this move.

Despite being so confident, I must admit that at one point, I began to feel unsure. I felt convinced that I would be better off staying in the job I had at the time. Compared with the uncertainty of moving to a country we had never seen, staying seemed more comfortable and secure. I even asked Christine to consider putting the application off. However, by then we had gone quite far in the process and there was no turning back. I let go of all my reservations and decided to stay on course.

After our papers were submitted to the Canadian High Commission in Kenya, we continued with our lives as normally as possible. Secretly we were anxious about the outcome. When we were all called to get our medicals, we were almost sure that we were going to get our visas. Thank God we had no medical issues, and this was a big blessing.

On June 26th, 2015, we received the email confirming the approval of our move to Canada, not just for Christine, but for all four of us. I was so excited and grateful for this opportunity to be together with my family in this new adventure. The boys were so thrilled and looked forward to all that Canada had to offer. We had only about one month to prepare to leave Kenya. Everything started rolling very fast. We had to sell all our personal and household belongings to give us enough money to settle in Canada. We saw God miraculously bring buyers for most of these items.

We arrived in Calgary, Alberta, Canada, on the 17th of August, 2015, and were welcomed warmly by my brother Ngala, his wife, Judy, and their kids. The Calgary airport was a three-hour drive from Medicine Hat, where Christine's college was. We spent the night in Medicine Hat. Christine registered at Medicine Hat College the following day. Then Ngala drove us two hours further east to Swift Current, Saskatchewan, where he lived.

Our arrival in Medicine Hat with Judy and Ngala's family

Checking into Medicine Hat College

We stayed in Swift Current for a couple of nights before Christine and I returned to Medicine Hat by Greyhound bus. We planned to look for a house and schools for the boys. Unfortunately, we did not know anyone in the city and had to ask around for everything. We were blessed to connect with a dear lady, Connie Grove, who gave us some ideas about schools and churches. Connie and her husband Joe became friends to my family and we enjoyed some good times together.

We visited a couple of schools before settling on Crestwood Elementary School for Matthew, who was going to start Grade 6, and Medicine Hat High School for Jonathan, who was to start Grade 9. We were told, however, that we could not register them without a local address and at that time our only address was in Swift Current.

Getting a house was imperative and it had to be within the school zone. Within a week we signed a lease for an apartment in the Crestwood area. We returned to Swift Current excited about having these two critical items in place and looking forward to living in Medicine Hat as a family.

The next week, we were back in Medicine Hat with the boys and our few pieces of luggage, ready to settle down and begin our new life in Canada.

Since we did not have much time before schools and college started in September, we bought only basic furniture. Then we needed clothes that would keep us warm and comfortable during the winter. We had never experienced winter before and were curious to know what this felt like. Everyone told us that some days were so cold, it was like being in a freezer. The only things that we managed to find and bring from Kenya were jackets and thermals from some flea markets. Later we discovered that they were quite outdated and not warm enough for the harsh prairie winter.

On our first Sunday in Medicine Hat, we visited a local church we had been told about, Hillcrest Evangelical Church. It was not as big as what we were used to back home, but people said that it was big for a community like Medicine Hat. We loved the worship, sermon and people who welcomed us so warmly.

It felt very similar to what we had in Kenya, so we decided to make this our home church. We felt it was important to get connected to the church where we hoped to serve God in some capacity. By connecting with people in this way we could build relationships and a support community for our family. We had learned from our church back home that it was important to connect and not merely sit around as consumers. Back in our home church Mavuno, I had served in the "Mizizi" Ministry and, along with Christine, had served as facilitators in the Family Ministry.

At Hillcrest, we started by joining a small group that met once a week called a "Life Group". Pastor Rob, who was in charge, asked me to co-lead this small group with my friend Miles Wright. We had very fulfilling and enriching times together during our Sunday evening meetings along with eight other individuals.

Then in the fall of 2016, our Pastor Jamie McDonald asked me to facilitate an inaugural class called "Starting Point" designed for those searching for faith. It would run every Tuesday evening for eight weeks. We felt so excited and honored to have this opportunity. About sixteen people came and some of them went on to form their own small Life Group. We were very encouraged by this. Also, we formed very strong friendships with some of the group—Marcus and Evie Coneys, Christy Borrisow, Larry and Janet Misson, and Jim French.

Hillcrest Church has continued to be a great support to me and my family throughout this journey with cancer. Many church members have taken time to visit with us, prepare meals, pray, encourage, and help with the boys' activities.

Settling down in Medicine Hat did not take too long. By getting connected to just a few people in church, we got to meet other people in and out of church. Since Medicine Hat is a small city of about sixty thousand people, it is not hard to meet a few people who know someone else you know.

My colleagues at Elm Street School, where I found a job, were also very warm and friendly. When I started working there, I did not have a car so I used the bus. Soon, one of the teachers, Joely Augustino, who lived not too far from my place, offered to give me a ride many times after school. She was always so cheerful and encouraging and many times challenged me to get out of my comfort zone.

During one of the men's fellowship meetings at Hillcrest Church, I met a great man of God, John Adegbenjo who was from Nigeria and was now living in Medicine Hat. He and his wife Felicia became good friends to Christine and I. They spent time to with us, prayed with us, encouraged us and met some practical needs of ours when we were new. Imagine our surprise when they told us that God had asked them to bless us with a vehicle. This was a huge blessing as we could not afford a vehicle at that time. John and Felicia have continued to be a blessing to our family through our journey offering a lot of spiritual support. Being from Africa, we have had lots to share in common and have enjoyed many days of laughter and encouragement in our various seasons.

Being away from home, especially during special holidays like Christmas, Thanksgiving and Easter, meant being alone as most of our family was far away in Kenya. These holidays back home meant lots of food, laughter and singing with family. We were so blessed to have friends in Medicine Hat who invited us to be with them during some of these holidays, thus making the holidays more like being at home. We had Christmas dinners with Regan Weeks' family, Joe & Joely's family and my good friends Ken and Lynn Klym. Occasionally we would drive to Swift Current or my brother would drive to Medicine Hat with his family to spend weekends and holidays together. I must admit that we were very blessed to have such good friends within such a short time of being in a new country.

There weren't many Kenyans in the city of Medicine Hat when we arrived. However, we did get to meet a few along the way and it was also a good time when we got together for a meal and some fun. We enjoyed eating

Kenyan food on such occasions and catching up with the latest happenings back home. Nicholas Langat became my good friend and 'brother from another mother'.

We also met a large community of Kenyans while staying in Calgary. Then through them, we met Kenyans in other parts of Alberta like Lethbridge, Duchess, Edmonton and Brooks. Within just one year we have connected with so many Kenyans and every time we meet, although we are in Canada, it becomes like an extension of home.

Celebrating Christine's graduation in June 2017

Picnic and retreat with Christine at Kin Coulee park in Medicine Hat, summer 2017

With Kenyan friends in Duchess, Alberta Canada, summer 2018
(L-R: Jonathan, Wycliffe, Felix and Philip)

CHAPTER 7:

HOW I BEAT CANCER

In order to catch your attention, I decided to call this chapter "HOW I BEAT CANCER." Why would this title catch your attention in a western culture? For one thing, you may know the end of the story. For another, this style of writing uses irony and sarcasm, which is common here. While I can write this way in Canada and it is completely acceptable in a literary work, it would not be highly regarded in the oral culture in Kenya. What I wish for is to beat cancer. It is what I would choose, but I know it's not completely up to me.

It all started in September of 2017. I took a road trip with one of my sons to Swift Current, Saskatchewan. We were going to visit my brother Ngala for the night. Before we left, we bought some snacks that included cashew nuts—which I love very much. When I got back to Medicine Hat, I noticed my left foot started to have small twitches. My first thought was that I had overeaten and was having a reaction to cashew nuts. I was sure, if I gave it time, it would go away. Unfortunately, it did not go away. It became progressively worse. Finally, I went to the emergency department to have my foot examined. All my tests were okay, and the doctor sent me home with a referral to a neurologist.

By the end of October, however, I was struggling to walk and had to drag my foot. This became extremely challenging at work because I was not able to keep up with the children that were in my care after school. I began to feel inadequate and inefficient in my performance at work. At home, my loving family was very supportive and did all they could to try to find a home remedy for these twitches. We checked YouTube for similar cases. There were various ailments such as drop foot, muscle cramps, too many cashew nuts, lack of magnesium, and overworked muscles, among others. We tried massaging the left foot and soaking it in Epsom salts. I tried simple exercises to relax my muscles. Again, unfortunately, none of these worked. I began to feel anxious and concerned.

A visit to my family physician did not yield any solutions either. He referred me to a nerve specialist for a nerve test. Nearing the end of October, I had not yet been contacted by the neurologist to whom I was referred. I went back to the emergency department. Walking had become very difficult and I was unstable. I was forced to buy a cane to help me maintain stability.

At this time, I began to feel extremely frustrated and fatigued whenever I walked. I started to minimize any movement so as to save energy and agony. The emergency doctor scheduled an MRI for December 7th and referred me to a neurologist in Medicine Hat. This neurologist called me almost immediately and set an appointment for November 20th, 2017. I left work early with much anticipation that finally a specialist would offer some relief. He examined me and made a referral to the hospital for a CT scan to be done immediately.

By this time my left arm had become weak and was hanging limp. I was advised not to go home until the results from the CT scan were ready. I sat waiting. I tried to relax, imagining that a solution would finally be found, and I would be treated. To my bewilderment, the results were just the opposite.

My doctor told me that a mass had been sighted in the right side of my brain. He also told me that I was being admitted to hospital right away and that I should call my wife to come and pick up our car.

I felt utter shock as I called Christine to give her this news. She called some friends to ask them to take her to the hospital immediately. The doctors talked to us, saying that the mass in the brain was likely a tumor requiring urgent attention.

After this diagnosis several calls were made to the neurologist at Foothills Hospital in Calgary to determine the next course of action. I was to be transferred to Calgary where surgery would be performed.

Everything was spinning so fast by this time, I felt like I was having a bad dream. We were told that they would only know whether the tumor was benign or malignant after a biopsy was done and analyzed. Enormous fears were triggered in me as I thought of the possibility of a cancer diagnosis.

I was scheduled for an MRI the following morning to gather pictures of the tumor. It was the longest night I have ever had in my life. Christine stayed with me all night and I could see the anxiety and shock on her face as she pondered what it could potentially mean for our family. The friends that accompanied her reassured her and other friends ensured that the children were okay at home.

The following morning the MRI was performed.

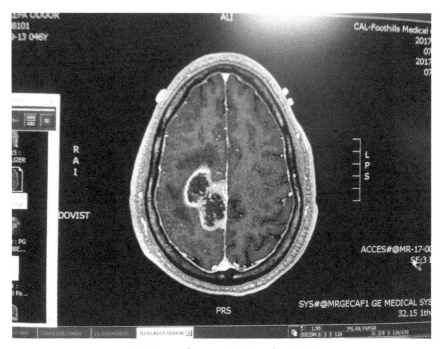

MRI scan of tumor in November 2017

My transfer to Calgary was the next priority. The doctors in Medicine Hat Hospital managed to get a bed for me at Foothills Hospital. By 12 pm I was being wheeled into an ambulance and taken to the airport for air transfer to Calgary. As we chatted with the friendly EMS crew, some of my anxious thoughts were diverted. However, Christine had to find her own way to Calgary after arranging for the boys to stay with good friends.

The next day, we were introduced to the neurosurgeon who was going to perform the surgery. He came to my bedside and had a candid talk with Christine and I. He explained the reason for the twitches in my foot and weakness in my left arm and leg. He said the tumor was located on the right frontal lobe and it was pressing, possibly damaging, some nerves that controlled the mobility on the left side of my body.

He gave us possible options moving forward. One was to do a biopsy to determine if the tumor was benign or malignant. He could also do a complete resection of the tumor through invasive surgery and afterwards examine the tumor. He also gave us the option of not having surgery. Either way mobility was going to be significantly affected. With surgery there was also the possibility of paralysis on the left side.

Christine and I opted for the surgery and the resection of the tumor. I was immediately put on the emergency waiting list for surgery. I waited for approximately seven days for my surgery. There always seemed to be another dire case that had to be attended to first. During this time, I experienced a lot of anxiety with raging thoughts of how my life would be after the operation. I thought about my career and how that would be impacted if I lost speech or had depleted cognitive abilities. The very thought of not being able to work again was devastating. The neurosurgeon allayed some of these fears by confirming this surgical procedure had a ninety-five percent chance of success with minimal impact on speech and cognition.

At last the day of surgery arrived on November 28th, 2017. Early in the morning I was prepared for the operating theater. Christine and her friend Kloie, were by my side. Kloie, a professional photographer, was there to take pictures of my preparation before surgery. I recall her taking a few video clips and asking me questions about how I felt that morning. For a moment, the anxious thoughts disappeared as I savored the attention of the video recording and pictures. I felt like a star. We were introduced to the surgical team that included two neurosurgeons and several nurses. The lead surgeon explained the surgery would take approximately three hours and another hour for preparation. During the operation, the tumor was going to be examined to determine if it was benign or malignant.

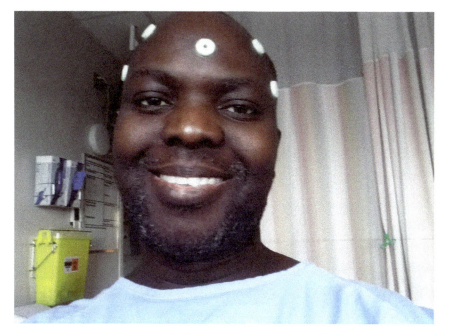

Preparing for brain surgery, November 2017

That morning, I had read from Psalm 121 in my devotions. It was a great assurance that God was my helper in this critical moment. Christine said a brief prayer over me to help calm my nerves. I abandoned myself totally to my Father in Heaven and felt some peace that all would be well as He would never leave me or forsake me.

I woke up recovering from the whole ordeal and found myself in a clean, white-walled ward. I was told this was the recovery ward and I was so glad to be alive. I began to feel like my body parts were coming back together. The following day, I waited in anticipation for the doctor to come in to examine me and give a report on my tumor. He came and explained everything to Christine and me. First, he confirmed the surgery was successful in that he was able to remove most of the tumor as far as the naked eye could see. That was such a relief for me.

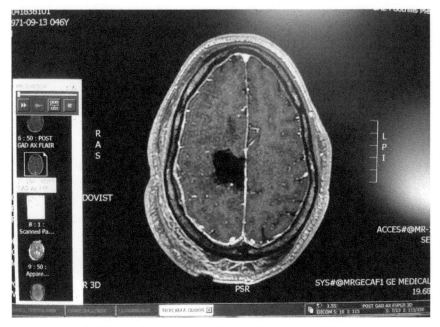

MRI scan after surgery, 2017; complete resection of tumor

What came as a horrible blow was that the tumor was malignant. He named it glioblastoma, Stage 4. He described it further as being one of the most aggressive brain tumors. We were devastated as we had hoped that cancer would never be a part of our lives. Christine had so many questions, while I remained silent, trying to take in the information. She asked if there was a possibility of it recurring anywhere else in my body. He informed us that this type of tumor only affects the brain and would be more likely to develop in some other part of the brain rather than metastasize to other parts of the body. I wasn't sure what would be better but the thought of having this ugly tumor in my life was simply horrifying, to say the least.

There it was. My diagnosis. The day my entire life turned upside down.

I guess I was in shock for quite a while as I pondered this information. What was to come next? The neurosurgeon explained that I would need to undergo intensive radiation and chemotherapy. This was aimed at killing any tumor cells that may have been left undetected during surgery and also preventing any further growth.

Intense emotions flooded me. The most significant feeling was fear because he told me that the prognosis for this type of cancer was about fifteen to eighteen months. That to me was like a death sentence.

Who would take care of and mentor my two boys? Would I live to see them graduate from high school and college? See them get married and have children?

I also did not want to leave my wife behind and I remembered my wedding vows, "till death us do part." Dying meant parting. I was scared!

I felt angry, too. What had I done to deserve this? All my life I had tried to be a good person. I never smoked, I never drank alcohol, and I did not have a wild life. (That was our definition of being good while growing up.) Why do such bad things happen to good people? That was my biggest question.

The doctors told me to enjoy my life as much as possible. I feared to die while wanting to live.

A few days after my surgery, I started physiotherapy and occupational therapy. It was intended to rehabilitate me and get me back on my feet. While I was still at Foothills Hospital in Calgary, I was wheeled down to the physio department on the third floor where I got therapy for about thirty minutes per session. This helped a great deal as I slowly began to regain use of my left side. Within a week of surgery, I was able to stand and take a few steps. I also began training my left arm to function again by using it to feed and dress myself instead of using my right hand, which is my dominant hand. I was told that I needed to use my left side as much a possible so that my brain could begin rewiring itself to regain functionality on this side. They called it neuroplasticity. This was difficult. It did not come easily for me and others had to keep reminding me to use the left side instead of the right.

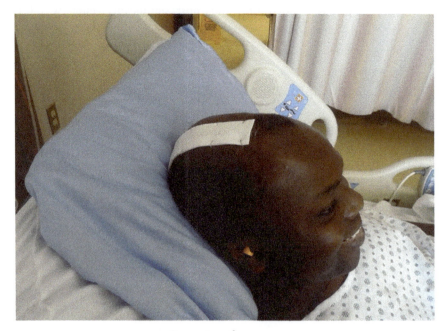

Recovering after surgery

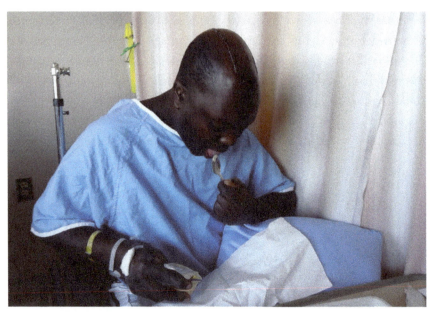

Rehabilitation: re-learning to eat with my left arm

I was anxious to see the new MRI scan after surgery. The neurosurgeon had indicated that the surgery was successful with a complete resection of the tumor as far as the human eye could detect. Indeed, the scan that was done post-surgery revealed just that. Now instead of a big mass, there was only a cavity. I found this quite encouraging. However, the doctor did not give any reassurance of full recovery nor did he say the tumor would not recur.

I was taken back to Medicine Hat Regional Hospital. On December 17th 2017, I was discharged from the hospital. This left me with less than a week to be at home for Christmas with my family. My mother-in-law had arrived from the USA to be with us for a month. This was such a blessing as she was able to stay with the boys for a couple of weeks while Christine and I were in Calgary.

We had just moved into a new house at the beginning of December and I had missed all that, including seeing what the new house looked like. I was therefore pleasantly surprised to find a beautifully decorated house with all our furniture positioned as if we had lived there for a while. Our friends Miles, Leanne, Cathi, and Brian had organized the move from our apartment on Crestwood Drive to the new house on Ross Glen Drive. Other Life Group and church members put up a lovely Christmas tree and decorated the house. This made me feel so loved and cared for. It was God's way of reminding me that He is in control and was taking care of my family.

Some of our Life Group members visiting at the Medicine Hat Regional Hospital

On Christmas Eve, my friend Ken and his wife Lynn invited our whole family for Christmas Eve dinner at their house. We were worried about how I would get down their stairs, but I managed somehow, and we enjoyed a lovely dinner together. Then on Christmas Day we spent the morning at home with mom, opening our gifts and making merry. So many friends had blessed our family with gifts knowing what we were going through. Reverend Lisa Waites and the St Andrew's parish in Bow Island had a load full of gifts for each of us. The staff at Christine's office also had their share of gifts. My work colleagues were not left behind. Led by Nikki and Emma, they made sure that we had very practical gifts to make us feel warmly welcomed as we settled into the new home. This was the first Christmas I had ever had such a large bundle of gifts from friends. It made it so special and uplifting despite all that we were facing.

Our living room with lovely Christmas tree and gifts, December 2017

Opening some of my gifts, Christmas 2017

Later that day, we were invited to Joely and Joe's home for dinner. Their house is just a few steps away from ours. It was such a joyous time being with friends who cared enough to share this day with us. Joely knew we were to travel to Calgary the following day and did not want us to have to bother cooking or doing any dishes. She had prepared a lovely meal for us to share. This was such a blessing to us.

On December 26th, 2017, Cathi and Brian Post from our Life Group arrived to help carry some of our luggage to Calgary. We had a lot because we were going to be there for six weeks and the boys were to be with us for about two weeks. They were on Christmas break from school and we did not want to leave them behind. Christine's mom came up with us, too, as she was scheduled to travel back to the US the following day. We therefore needed an extra car that could carry all our combined luggage.

We were so blessed to have a contact from church with a family in Calgary who were willing to host us while I underwent treatment there. Lisa and her husband Lucian had a beautiful home with a large basement suite, which they offered to us at no charge and as a ministry to God. Christine had stayed with them previously while I was in hospital. This was indeed a blessing to us as accommodation in Calgary is quite expensive. My only challenge about staying there was getting up and down the winding staircase to the basement. By this time, I was not as strong as I had been when I left Calgary after surgery. I had to have both Jonathan and Lucian help me get up or down. I came to realize that the increased weakness was due to increased inflammation in the brain after surgery.

I checked in to the Tom Baker Cancer Centre in Calgary on December 27th, 2017, to begin thirty sessions of radiation therapy and daily chemotherapy for six weeks. The doctor on duty immediately increased the steroid dose I was taking in order to reduce the inflammation in my brain. After a few days I had begun to feel better, and I was even planning to go back to Medicine Hat over the first weekend of January when Christine drove the boys back. They needed to prepare for school, which would start in the second week of January.

Waiting for first radiation treatment, December 2017

Jonathan, my right-hand support as I attended treatment

Unfortunately, on the day we were to travel, I received an urgent call from the Tom Baker Cancer Centre. They informed me that my blood sugar had spiked to 36 and I should report to the nearest emergency department. We abandoned the trip and went straight to the Foothills Hospital's emergency department. I was admitted that night in order to get my sugar levels stabilized.

After a few days in hospital, the doctors decided that I was safer staying there and having my radiation and chemotherapy done from there. My mobility and transfers had become a challenge for Christine alone now that

Jonathan had to go back to school and Lucian was back work. Christine continued to stay at Lisa's house and spent the days with me at the hospital.

We were blessed to have a good friend, Brad Dilman, who offered to drive up from Medicine Hat and pick up the boys. He was also willing to stay with them at home so that they did not need to move out of the house to stay with friends while we were away for treatment. This was a big relief for Christine as she did not have to drive back to Medicine Hat in the winter. All she had to do was organize a way for the boys to still be able to attend their activities during the week.

Being so far away from home meant that I had to rely more on friends to take care of my family. I thought about how it would have been if I was in the same situation in my home country, Kenya. Back home, with so many family members around, we probably would have had less concern about the boys because there would always have been someone for them to stay with. I was so glad that God had blessed us with such a good support network in Canada. Many new friends offered us transportation, food and accommodation for the boys.

After I was admitted into hospital for control of blood sugar, I was put on a diabetic diet and given insulin injections. I continued to undergo my radiation sessions and was wheeled from my room to the radiation unit, which was housed adjacent to the Foothills Hospital.

The boys visiting me in hospital

During my stay at the hospital, I was granted a weekend pass that allowed me to go out of the hospital while still being in-patient. I was looking forward to a break from the hospital and to some fresh air outside. The weekend we chose to go out was one when our boys were playing soccer in a town called Okotoks, which was just about forty minutes away from Calgary. I was looking forward to going to watch them play for their Medicine Hat team, RASC. Wycliffe Oduor offered to drive us down to Okotoks and back. It was a rainy and cloudy day. Because Wycliffe lived in Calgary, he was used to maneuvering through the speeding traffic and the trip went well.

Watching the boys play soccer in Okotoks, Alberta, February 2018

Due to challenges with my mobility, a Kenyan family we had met during our time there, kindly offered to host us at their house, which did not have stairs. Damaris and Joseph Mutua opened their home to our family, including our boys, so they were able to spend a night with us after their Okotoks soccer tournament.

During that weekend, there was a fellowship held at the Mutuas' home by a Kenyan group called 'Ombeni Group'. We were glad to be part of their fellowship that Sunday afternoon and I must admit it felt so much like being back in Kenya. We got to meet a lot more Kenyans that day, many of whom have become good friends.

I was glad when my last radiation session finally ended on February 7th, 2018. I felt a big sense of relief as I said farewell to the friendly staff in the radiation department. Tom Baker Cancer Centre has a tradition where a patient who successfully completes treatment rings 'The Bell of Hope' three times after their last session. This is met with joyous claps from everyone in the vicinity in celebration of hope for the patient who has completed treatment. My wife stood by my side as I rang that bell with so much hope in my heart. I had made it through the grueling six weeks under that machine. I hoped that my life would go back to normal.

The Bell of Hope at Tom Baker Cancer Centre

Now it was time to go back to Medicine Hat where I was to recuperate for a month before resuming another cycle of chemotherapy. This time the chemotherapy would be for only five days with a rest of twenty-three days before starting another cycle. The best part was that I could take the pills orally from the comfort of my own home. I only went to Calgary once a month for blood work and an assessment with my oncologist.

Settling back at home was a challenge as so many changes had to be made to accommodate my needs. Christine and some friends went to Red Cross and AJ's Loan Cupboard for equipment that was needed for my comfort and safety.

Rehabilitation for my left side recommenced in Medicine Hat. I had been given a knee brace to prevent my left knee from snapping while I walked. Later I received a custom-made foot brace for my left foot that was designed both to raise my foot and also to assist my walking. I had a team of therapists who came to the house and helped me with some range of motion exercises, household tasks and walking. Initially I seemed to benefit but, over time, it became increasingly difficult to lift my leg high enough to get over one stair level or even walk around the house. The physiotherapy sessions were gradually reduced as I continued to become weaker on my left side.

Two of my brothers, Ngala on my right and Buore on my left, visiting me at home

In April 2018, after completing two cycles of chemotherapy, I suddenly began to experience tremors in my left hand again. I noticed that my left side was weaker. I started having sharp headaches. At that point Christine took me to emergency to see a doctor. A specialist was called in to assess. He confirmed that the tremors were localized seizures and immediately he put me on anti-seizure medication.

Around April 2018, I also had a third MRI. Some new growth of the tumor was detected. This came as an even bigger shock to me than the initial diagnosis. I was hoping that none of this was true. I could not imagine having anther tumor in my brain.

A visit back to my oncologist in Calgary at the end of May 2018 confirmed this as well. He felt that with my increased weakness, taking chemotherapy was going to be counterproductive and would leave me too depleted. He therefore put a hold on further cycles of chemotherapy. Christine asked what other options were open for me especially regarding clinical trials and new therapies in the market. He did not know of any. He even went on to say that even if there were some clinical trials, I would not qualify due to my physical limitations. I went back home quite dejected but still praying and believing God for a miraculous healing. I was then referred to palliative care in Medicine Hat.

While at home, I was receiving home care from Alberta Health Services. Health care aides would come in in the morning and evening to wash and dress me for the day. In the evening, they came to get me ready for the night. During the day, they would come in for two to three hours and help me with my medication and lunch. They called it respite. During this time, Christine went to work or ran errands. I worried for her as she was doing so much for me at home. I knew she needed time for herself, too.

Visiting with Ngala's family from Swift Current and Janet (Buore's wife) from the US

Eventually, caring for me at home became increasingly difficult. The workers feared handling me on their own and insisted always on a second person to ensure my safety. In August 2018, my legs began to give way easily and I had a couple of falls. My last fall landed me back in the Medicine Hat Hospital. I was admitted following shortness of breath. A CT scan of my chest revealed two massive blood clots. I was lucky to be alive. I was immediately started on blood thinners, which I will have to take for the rest of my life.

After about two weeks in hospital, a case conference was called to plan for my transition from hospital. This conference was composed of the lead doctor from the Cancer Clinic, two palliative doctors, a transition nurse, physio and occupational therapists and the social worker from the Cancer Clinic. They felt that since I did not require acute care at the hospital, they needed a transition plan to ensure that I would get the best possible care.

Given the nature of my unique physical needs, they decided it safer for me to be admitted at the St. Joseph's Covenant Home. We were told that the facility had special auxiliary beds for intermediate care. It also housed the palliative unit including hospice beds, which were typically for end of life care.

Enjoying fall weather in the gardens at St. Joe's, September 2018

I was promised that I could get a day pass to go home whenever I felt up to it. I was keen to see the facility and from the start I was quite accepting of it. It was comfortable, clean and had friendly staff. I got my own room with my own bathroom, something that I value a lot while in a hospital. Since walking was quite a struggle for me, the facility used a lift to move me around.

I did not mind the transition since I hoped it would just be a short while before I was able to go back home. I therefore decided to write my memoir and make the most of my free time at the facility. With time, the writing became labored and Christine had to write or type as I dictated.

As I write this memoir, I have many questions and many anxious thoughts. I also continue to trust in Jesus my Savior, who has the ultimate power to heal and restore me fully. I am confident that my life is secure in the One who holds the universe in His hands. He has the final say on my life and either way, I win!

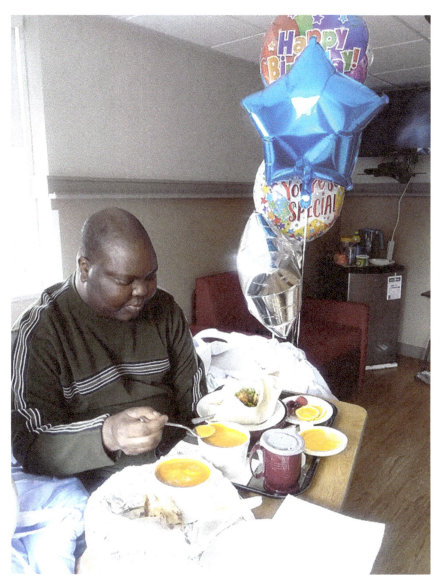

My special lunch on my 47th birthday at St. Joseph's, September 13th, 2018

My family made my 47th birthday at St. Joseph's special, September 2018

My brother-in-law Karimi and his wife Wambui visited from the US, October 2018

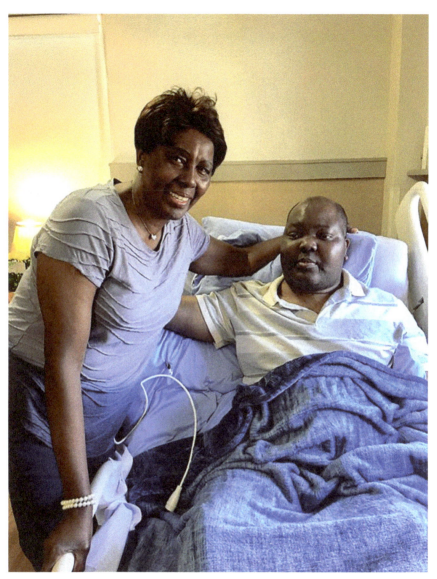

With my Mom-in-law visiting from US in October 2018

With Jim and Geneva Burk visiting with us in October 2018

With my sister Betty visiting from the US with niece Nelly, October 2018

CHAPTER 8:

CHANGES

Since I got this diagnosis, my life has changed significantly in many areas.

Physical Strength and Mobility – Ever since my first tremors in my life foot, my left side began to weaken. I sincerely hoped that the surgical removal of the tumor would restore my mobility. Unfortunately, it did not. I started using a cane, then a walker and eventually a wheelchair. It became increasingly difficult to stand or walk a few steps. At home, Christine would insist that I walk from my recliner seat to the dining table for meals. At first it was okay, but with time, I hated it so much I would have rather stayed hungry. Walking had become like climbing a mountain. Getting in and out of the car was strenuous and any trip away left me completely exhausted.

Freedom to Drive – November 20th, 2017, was the last time I drove a vehicle. From this day forward, I was advised not to drive. Things worsened after I began to experience a partial seizure in May of 2018. Not being able to drive meant that I was totally dependent on others. Losing my independence was very painful for me. I felt an enormous and crushing sense of loss.

Extra Equipment for Daily Living – I stayed in the hospital for a month after my surgery. When I returned home, we had to make many adjustments to accommodate my problems with mobility. I had to get a knee brace to prevent my left knee from snapping as I walked. I also had to get a raised toilet seat, bathroom rail, bath chair and a bed rail. Basically, I needed a lot more support to ensure my safety during the performance of tasks that are basic functions of everyday life. This sometimes was very frustrating and inconvenient. I felt sad for Christine as she had to go and rent this equipment from the Red Cross and AJ's Loan Cupboard in Medicine Hat. The occupational therapist at the Medicine Had Hospital was kind enough to direct us to places where we could find all the equipment I needed at home.

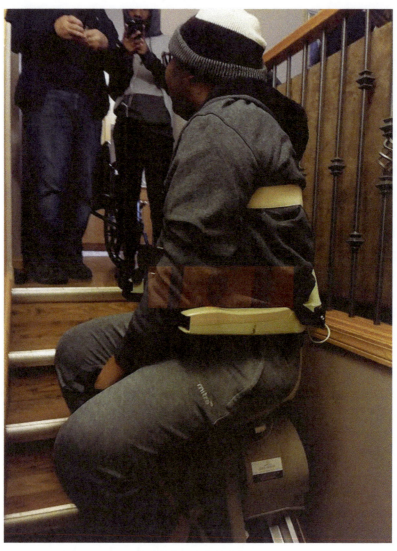

Stair lift installed at home

Losing the Big Bedroom – We planned to move into a new home in November of 2017. I recall my sons fighting to get the biggest room in the basement. However, my wife put her foot down saying this was to be the master bedroom. To get into the house, one has to either go upstairs to the main floor, or downstairs to the basement.

After my arrival back home in December, I had to get used to climbing up and down the staircases. In time it became increasingly difficult to walk down the stairs to go to bed. Painfully, I had to sacrifice our large bedroom and switch rooms with our son who had a bedroom upstairs. This room, though much smaller, was going to restrict my movements to one floor, making it much easier for me. Again, my lovely wife managed to get help from good friends to make this change possible. This was a big relief for me.

Enforced Diet – Often people change their diet when cancer strikes. I was no exception. I loved eating well and, formerly, I enjoyed a lot of fast food. This is not to say that it caused the tumor. However, it was safer to change my diet to healthier food.

Christine bent over backwards to ensure that I had fresh fruits and vegetables daily. She eliminated all sugar from my diet and her support in this was a great encouragement to me. Of course, I had my cheat days that would send me on a guilt trip after my blood sugar would spike to very high levels. It took a while for me to adjust to this new diabetic diet and I still struggle to eat and drink certain things. I knew that doing this was for my own health, but I still grieved the loss of freedom to eat whatever I liked.

Body Image – The unpleasant change in my body was my weight. I gained a new shape. Before the surgery I weighed about 91 kilograms. As of September 2018, I weighed about 115 kilograms because of the steroid medication I have been taking since surgery. The drug Decadron makes one feel very hungry and I wanted to eat all the time. My reduced mobility made my lifestyle very sedentary and I retained a lot of weight. As a result of these changes my clothes' size went up. The steroid also had the effect of distending my belly. It resembled a keg and stuck out more than usual. My face became puffy with lots of fluid retention. Sometimes my feet were so puffed and swollen that I could not wear my normal shoes. I could only wear Crocs. This weight gain also made it more difficult to maneuver and by July 2018, I needed two people to assist me in walking and getting to bed. On two occasions, I found myself on the floor requiring three men to help me get up. I hated this feeling of being totally dependent on others.

Independence in Self Care – The most profound change that affected me was the change in my independence. After I left Calgary in February 2018, I came home needing support not just from my wife but also from health care aides who came to our home. They helped me get ready for the day and for bed at night. I lost all privacy. I was not accustomed to being bathed, taken to the bathroom or having help to get dressed. At first, I found it very embarrassing but with time I accepted all the help I could get. One of the friends who has been a big help in getting me to appointments has been Pete Rose. With mobility becoming a challenge, I needed more than just Christine and Jonathan to get me around safely. Pete assisted again and again to ensure that I was safe during my transfers.

Role as Husband and Father – I would say that my wife is my angel. She has taken on roles that she would not have taken if I were healthy. I used to drive my boys to their extracurricular activities both in and out of town. Now I was rendered unable. For a while Christine had to depend on friends to take the boys to their activities while she was with me for my treatment in Calgary. I used to take care of all car maintenance and bill payments but now Christine is graciously doing all these tasks. I am forever grateful for such a loving, loyal and committed wife. This to me has been God's way of helping me adjust to this significant change in my life.

I will always be grateful as well, to the many friends who cared for our boys while I was away for treatment. Friends like Nicholas Langat, Yusuf Mohammed, Marcus and Evie Coneys who hosted our boys while we were away in Calgary. Miles and Leanne Wright, Leanne Stanke and many others faithfully ensured my boys made it to their soccer practices, games and other activities. Brad Dilman became my right-hand man for many of our household repairs and vehicle issues. Another special friend, Chuck Nelson, ensured that our lawn was well manicured by getting us a mower and ensuring its maintenance. He was there to re-train the boys so that they did a good job mowing the lawn.

Moving Out of My Home into a Care Home –I guess the ultimate blow for me was being transferred to the St. Joseph's Covenant Home. Initially the plan was to transition to one of auxiliary beds in the facility with the hope of going back home once I regained my strength. I was at risk of falling at home and it was no longer safe for Christine to attempt to care for me on her own at home. At St. Joseph's, I received 'round-the-clock nursing care with a doctor's check-in daily to monitor my progress. I loved the environment and nursing staff who were so caring and friendly.

My physio session at St. Joe's

With my mobility team: Pete Rose, Jonathan and Matthew, November 2018

CHAPTER 9:

REFLECTIONS FROM A HOSPICE ROOM

The following thoughts are reproduced verbatim from Kefa's conversation with Natalie Oliphant on September 17th, 2018.

Christine

I knew the minute I met Christine that she would be the one I would marry.

I remember my retreat with Christine in Kenya.

When you become emotional, you become closer.

I need to know what makes my wife Christine happy. I need to know her needs. Would flowers make her happy? I have not sent her flowers. When we owned a flower business, I did not want a florist who was our competitor to send her flowers. I did not want her to arrange her own flowers from me. Ladies often bought flowers for themselves. What does Christine long for? Food? Flowers?

Food is a love language.

Food shows love and enjoyment. This is how my mother showed love.

Laughter is a common language. A smile is too.

Jonathan and Matthew

Jonathan's birthday was held downstairs yesterday. Fifty people came. What advice do I give to my eighteen-year-old son?

Abstinence and being faithful when in young relationships.

Teach children to be obedient to authority. Life expectancy is higher if you are careful.

A lift has been installed in our home, so now I can go for a visit and interact with my children.

Always teaching our children. Always adjusting their ingredients. Add a little salt until you get the right taste. Leave something that tastes good.

Pizza with Jonathan: Jonathan will take my car to get pizza and we will eat too much. But right before the pizza is in our mouths Christine calls to ask me about my blood sugar. She has unfathomable timing.

Chicken and a movie ticket.

Work

We were not in the business of selling flowers. We were in the business of improving relationships.

Marketing is about needs, not sales.

In a boardroom you get one vote per person. In my community, will my vote influence politics? Fact of life. A vote is a vote and it affects everyone. Everyone counts. Every job counts.

We are one person away from the person we want to meet. Could be a connection.

Health

My doctor gave me chocolate. She said to enjoy life as much as I can.

Why do objects in the rear-view mirror seem larger than they appear? Same with the tumor scan.

I have a friend from Kenya that passed away this morning. He was on dialysis. And another friend with cancer passed away as well.

Most significant events of this day: today two friends have passed. I ask myself what will happen to me. I am worried and scared, and I do not want to imagine what can happen to me. Am I in a worse condition?

As my friends have passed on, I wonder who will be next. The person in the next bed might be next.

I have an arsenal box in my fridge. Christine wants me to have my health longer than my sickness. She keeps my walker far away to keep me from the fridge and the sweets inside. She hears the first sound of the walker if I am going to get a treat.

It's hard to know if I have a family history of cancer. There was no diagnosis in Kenya. No people were being tested for it.

Sitting on this bed going through the effects of cancer causes me to ask myself who is next? And what kind of legacy am I leaving?

What People Say

"How are you?" is a greeting. "Fine," is the reply, but if you are not fine, will the person come back and ask?

An Alberta health care worker came in and asked me, "Do you know you are going to die?" I thought, "You are going to die too." It is an appointment no one will miss.

Kenya

I remember we went to a fellowship meeting with friends. The last couple to arrive was followed by a gang of thugs. We lay on the floor. They hit us with the butts of their pistols. Women are stronger than men. A woman with a child asked them not to kill us but to go upstairs to ransack the bedrooms. Everyone was instructed to remove their rings. My ring came off easily even though it was usually snug on my finger. Christine refused to give her ring to them. She hid it under the sofa until they were gone. To this day I have no wedding ring. Christine's commitment is so strong. *[Note: Refer to the end of Chapter 4 and a mention of a new wedding ring, a gift from Christine on their 20th wedding anniversary, December 5th, 2018.]*

In Kenya you must keep your hands on the dashboard when stopped by police officer. They cannot be concealed. Don't take chances with this.

I remember my high school playing "Chariots of Fire" all day. It was also my brother's wedding march.

Miss Survanah, my French teacher at our all-boys high school, taught us to always look into the eyes. Eyes to the soul. She would wear a 'sari' with a bare stomach. One of the boys touched her stomach.

Canada

The new looks old with one wash. Canada is wasteful.

So much waste. Water. We don't need new clothes.

I have had more privileges than my friends in Kenya. Facilities in Kenya are substandard, different than in Canada. Kenya is a developing country; I appreciate Canada.

I am privileged.

Something supernatural allowed me to come to Canada.

I benefit from this medical system.

Excellent service here.

This is a good facility. I have a good level of comfort. 4:00 pm food is served and I enjoy it. I don't compare it to a developing country. Thank God I am here currently. The care is amazing.

There are no restrictions in this place. I enjoy time spent with my family.

What Matters

Appearance matters, no matter who you are. How you dress shows a culture.

Nature prepares us for leaving home. Eagles allow their eaglets to fall. They take them to higher places and let them fall in order to soar.

Memories look bigger than they actually are. It's how you look at life. What is important?

On a bus it doesn't matter where you are seated; people exit, and you don't know who will be next. It is the bus of life. I do lots of soul-searching about who is next. The driver is always waiting. The driver of this bus is God.

Die to be alive for Jesus.

We need to live each day. Do we leave people happier or in a worse situation? How have you made someone else's life better today? Have you changed someone's life today?

Godly legacy.

You decide when to stop your memoir.

Heaven is a beautiful place.

CHAPTER 10:

LOVING WORDS AND THOUGHTS FROM GEORGE DAVISON ELEMENTARY SCHOOL

The following thoughts are reproduced verbatim from Kefa's work colleagues at George Davison Elementary School. They gifted him with a lovely book titled "Beautiful Hands" in which they penned these sincere thoughts for Kefa in November 2018.

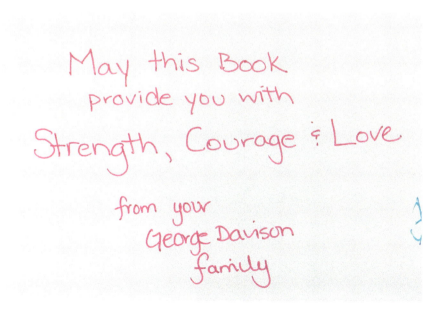

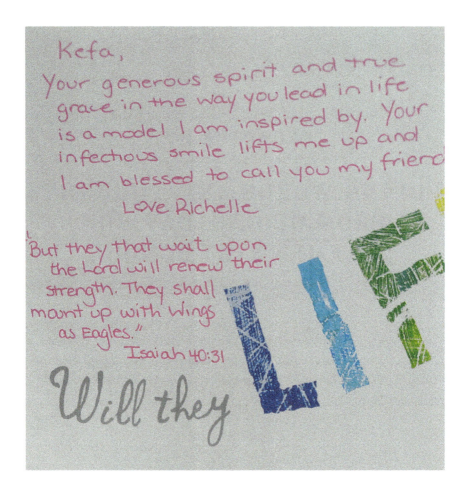

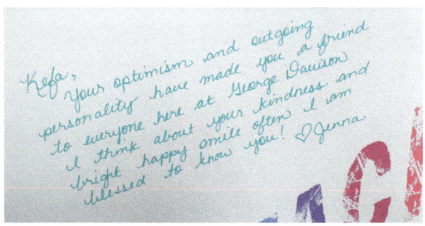

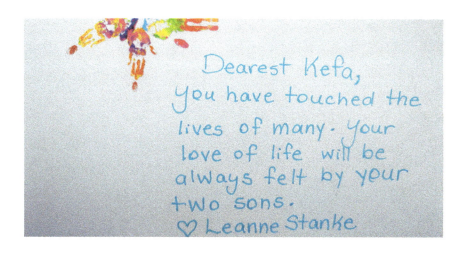

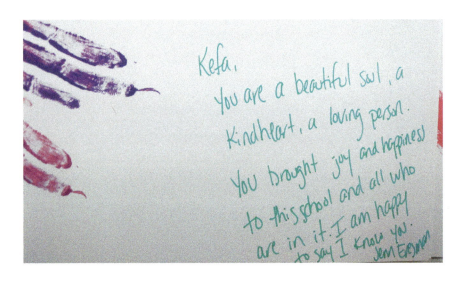

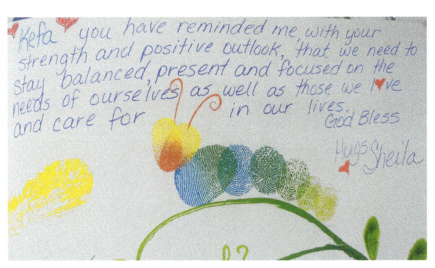

CHAPTER 11:

EPILOGUE

Christine Oduor

"Legacy is about life. About the times we've lived in,
the people and events that have helped shape us,
how and whom we've loved,
what has stirred us, and how we've tried.
When there's been laughter and where the tears have come—
those times are here, too."
Linda Spence

"Legacy is preparing those you love to grow
through life's most difficult challenges."
Tom Ziglar

Kefa Oduor Tuju continued to battle for his life into December 2018. December was not an easy month for him as he had totally lost the use of his left side. Despite this difficult phase, he had one thing that kept him going, and that was documenting his legacy in this book he was writing.

Then one week into December when his physiotherapist came in for the weekly session, it became painfully clear that it had become difficult for Kefa to stand on his feet anymore. We could see that he was desperately willing to walk, but his will could no longer override the affected parts of his brain.

The physiotherapist assessing him called off the session, saying that it was not wise to push him further.

It was on this Thursday afternoon that she sadly and gently let me know that she did not think that it was going to be practical for her to continue with the sessions because Kefa was not responding positively but was instead deteriorating physically.

This news pierced my heart sharply; I felt like my life was being deflated. It was very painful to hear as this meant that Kefa could no longer come home on a Sunday day pass. I knew he was not going to like this outcome and I did not want to have to be the one to disseminate this news to him. We agreed that the physiotherapist would talk to the hospice doctor and that the doctor would communicate to Kefa on Sunday when he came around that morning.

Fortunately, the next Sunday that came along, December 9th, Kefa slept in. He was not up early as usual. It was as if he did not even realize it was Sunday. One look at his face and I could tell that he was quite tired, even though he had slept pretty much the whole night. It was as if the disease was beginning to wear him out.

By this time, I noticed a small bump on his head on the right side. That was the side that had the tumor removed and it seemed, as the scans had revealed, the tumor was growing to the point of pushing out through the skull. At least that was the thought in my mind. He did not raise any issue with it as it was not hurting him in any way, but it disturbed me a lot. I tried to cheer him up and avoided discussing anything about going home. When the doctor came in for his morning rounds, he also did not mention anything about going home for the day, so I decided to go with the flow.

Later , it dawned on Kefa that it was actually Sunday and he asked about going home. For a moment, I panicked, wondering what I would tell him. I was quick to say that since he slept in, I did not want to rouse him and with most of the day gone, it was best that we let the Sunday pass and stay in. I managed to convince him that I wanted us to put some finishing touches to the book before sending it off to a friend who was going to start editing. The boys came over and we spent the whole day with Kefa at the hospice trying to cheer him up.

The rest of the week was very tiring for Kefa. He did not get out of bed much. His mood was really low and it was a big struggle to get him to take his supplements. The new range of treatment using natural supplements was now my only hope of a turnaround. It was a regimen of timed pills three times a day. I was beginning to get frustrated as I wanted so badly for him to get better. I no longer had the patience or time to let the pills work. However, there were too many pills. I could see that Kefa did not seem very keen on taking so many pills in a day. I called the doctor's office in Ontario and told them how much it was becoming a struggle for Kefa to swallow the pills. They advised that I should try mixing the pills in applesauce, which was sweet and soft to swallow. It was all trial and error for me and I mustered all the effort I could to get him to comply. He complained of the pills being bitter and difficult to swallow even with the applesauce. I tried to convince him that this was the only way he was going to get better and that he needed to focus on that goal instead of the discomfort of the process. All my attempts to convince him seemed to fall on deaf ears. If anything, he appeared not to want to get better, at least in my eyes. I was relentless and made sure that there was always a trusted friend with him who could help give the pills if it was a time when I was at work.

As Christmas was approaching, some of our Life Group members came to visit and even put up some decorations in his room so as to cheer him up. Kefa was very happy and uplifted with the flashing lights, especially in the evening when the room was dark. I kept wondering to myself what Christmas was going to look like for us this year. It was very difficult to plan, but by this time, I was almost certain it was going to be a Christmas in the hospice. I tried not to think much about it being so dull and cold. I had really hoped that Kefa would be well enough to make it home at least on Christmas Day.

The following week seemed empty, with very little activity. Kefa had a companion (health care aide) who came to sit with him daily from 10 am to 2 pm. Usually, she would take him out for a walk/ride in his wheelchair, just in the compound or vicinity. There was a little café down the street that he had come to like for their hot beverages and pastry snacks. Other times, she tried other options to keep him engaged indoors. They played some board games in the games room downstairs and she also helped him read through his writing.

The week of December 10th was very cold outside and Kefa was not very enthusiastic about going out of the room. He preferred to stay in his room and preferred to lay in bed despite my promptings to get up and sit in his chair for a while. By this time, medical staff were not keen on having him sit in his wheelchair all by himself because his left side was very weak and made him tilt to the left, with the risk of a fall very high.

Kefa was looking forward to coming home on Sunday, December 16th, but I managed to convince him that we could go to church instead since he had not been to church in a while. He was very excited about this. I knew that a trip to church did not require him to leave his wheelchair and that after the service, we would head straight back to the hospice for him to rest.

Instead, that morning, he received many visitors and going to church was not an option. I was quite okay with that, too, because I could see that he seemed weak and the swelling on his head was getting bigger. By the time the last visitors left, Kefa was extremely exhausted from all the fun, laughter and talking. He was ready for bed early and I took the opportunity to go home early as well so that I could return to hospice early.

I was up early and ready for the day on Monday December 17th, 2018. I had also been called in to work that week to cover for someone who was on vacation. I had to plan my time very well on such days when I had to go to work. I started the day at the hospice by 7 am. and always made sure I gave Kefa some of his meds and helped with his breakfast before reporting to work at 8:15 am.

When I arrived that morning, he told me that he had a headache during the night and had been given some pain relievers. It was quite a struggle giving him his supplements that morning; he had difficulty swallowing them. I knew that he did not fancy taking all these pills and I thought he was just in one of those moods. I, on the other hand, was desperate for him to get better and tried all my best to gently help him swallow them.

Unfortunately, it did not work and he even threw up, sending me into a panic. I quickly buzzed the nurse and they assisted with cleaning him up. The nurse said that he needed to rest as it was difficult for him to swallow anything else. So, I headed out to work.

Soon after I left, he complained of more headaches and they continued to sedate him, hoping the headaches would subside and he would wake up and eat. But he never ate that whole day as he was asleep most of the day. He would only wake up to point at his head, his only way of communicating his pain. I was unable to see him during my lunch break as I had to attend my first counseling session with a counselor to whom we had been referred. The situation was becoming very heavy for me and I needed some professional help coping with it. I was not so worried as his companion was there to spend a good part of the day with him. All she briefed me was that he slept most of the day.

By the time I got back from work at 4 pm, I was very concerned about his state. The nurse on duty tried to console me, telling me that they were doing their best to make sure he was comfortable and free of pain, and that all that they could offer at this time was comfort care. She said that they had made another attempt at feeding him but he would not open his mouth to eat.

The last time he had had an episode like this one, which was about one and half months prior , he came around after one day. And so, with this incident, we could only hope that the morning would bring us hope of a turnaround again. This was all so heavy for me to handle alone. Fortunately, our dear friend Sue Braid offered to come and sit with Kefa and me in the room. She was by my side, ready to listen and give me a hug when I needed it.

Another big relief for me was when Kefa's brother, Ngala, arrived that Monday evening. He said he felt that he was prompted to come that evening all the way from Swift Current where he lived. He usually did not come to visit during the week, or on a Monday for that matter. I was happy that he was around and could spend the night with Kefa since I had to go home and be with the boys. I had so much going on for me that I made it a priority to go home and spend the night with the boys while getting myself a good night's rest. This enabled me to be fresh and energized for next day when I needed to be with Kefa at the hospice and my other activities.

By the evening, Kefa was still not talking and only made some gestures with his right hand towards his head. When he did this, we knew he was in pain and it was time for the next pain reliever (sedative). As much as these injections helped to relieve his pain, I was not happy because they made him even more drowsy and this meant that he could not communicate with us. The nurses stressed again that this was the only way to keep him comfortable. I was quite perturbed the whole night and was worried that something did not seem right. I went home considerably anxious that day. I kept praying and asking God to perform a miracle like He had done the last time and pull Kefa through this hurdle.

I was up the following morning and at the hospice by 7 am as usual. I had been praying and hoping for a turnaround by morning. I had asked for some time off work as Kefa was scheduled for an MRI at the regional hospital that morning and I had to be there to accompany him.

Unfortunately, that morning marked the day I never wanted to come in my whole life. The nurse attending to him did not seem very hopeful. She called me into a neighboring room for a chat. I obliged and quickly followed her, my anxious thoughts racing as I pondered what could be the matter. She had me sit down on the couch and sat across from me, her face as warm and calm as she usually was. Then, very gently, she told me that things were not looking good at all and they were sure Kefa would not make it for the MRI. Worse still, with the poise of a seasoned hospice nurse, she quietly said, "Kefa is in the active stages of dying." She went on to say that no one could tell how long he would be alive, so it was best for us to be by his side spending as much quality time with him as we could.

I felt like a bomb had just exploded in me; everything was spinning so fast. This was not what I was expecting and I was definitely not prepared to deal with this outcome! She reached out to hold my hand as she let me absorb the very difficult news. She took her time with me in the room and did not rush me to leave. However, as a matter of urgency, she advised me to pull the boys out of school and have them come to sit with their dad.

The most discouraging part of it was that because of the continued sedation, he was going to be comatose but could hear all that we were saying. This meant that there was no way we could talk and process what this meant for both of us. There was no way I was going to know what was going on in his mind and worse still, no way of him saying goodbye to us. Therefore, she encouraged us to keep talking to him even when he did not physically respond to us.

I was scheduled to report to work that morning after the MRI and, of course, I knew this was not going to happen, at least not for a long time.

Although I was in shock, I quickly called Ngala in to let him know what I had just been told. He did not say much. I knew that this was not the news he was expecting to hear either. He was scheduled to return home to Swift Current that day, but he postponed his return trip. He needed to be by his brother now and his brother needed him too. I sensed deep in my spirit that was why God had led him to come the previous night.

In hindsight, I feel it was as if Kefa was calling Ngala to be with him in his final moments—his own way of saying goodbye. Indeed, I knew the saying "blood is thicker than water" was very true. Ngala stayed by Kefa's side throughout and would only step out of the room when absolutely necessary. This gave me some relief, especially because I had to leave and pick the boys from school.

Immediately after I talked with Ngala, I called up my supervisor at work and told her what I had just been told. I had to excuse myself from the office as well. She burst into tears, crying for me. She did not know what to tell me because this was very painful to hear. She couldn't imagine what I was going through. This was really hard for me. She offered all the support that she could and sent one of my colleagues to the hospice right away.

What a relief when my colleague, Lorrie, arrived just in time to drive me to both schools to pick up the boys. I mustered up all the strength I could to explain to the administration why the boys had to leave. Since it was the last week of school before the Christmas break, it was highly unlikely that they would be returning before the break. Our biggest concern was that Jonathan was just about to complete his first semester of Grade 12, his final year of high school. He had to prepare for the Grade 12 Diploma exams coming up during the second week of January 2019. Now he would miss those prep classes. Quite frankly, at that moment, exams lost their priority. Now every moment the boys had with their dad was paramount.

Although Kefa was totally unresponsive by this time after being so heavily sedated, we spent the rest of the day by his side talking and holding his hands.

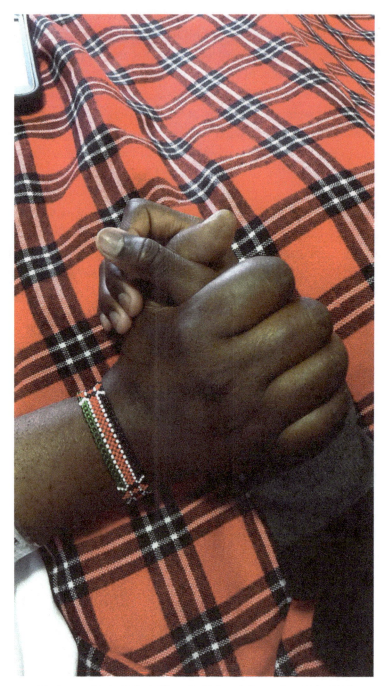

The boys at his bedside, holding Kefa's hand, December 18th, 2018

All we were told was that he could hear us and that it was important that we kept our conversations positive and cheerful. Many of our friends heard that he was not doing well and came to be with us by Kefa's side, also cheering him up. We needed all their support and prayers to see us through this difficult phase. The hospice staff very kindly provided us with refreshments and snacks. Friends filled up the room. Some had to sit in the adjacent room. How encouraging it was to have them around. It helped the boys and I feel like we were not alone. Some of our family members back home in Kenya were also preparing to come over.

As the evening wore on, I agonized over whether to spend the night with Kefa or at home. The medical team could not predict when he would go. They said, "It could be anytime, a day, a week or even two weeks." I felt so perplexed. Gradually a quiet calm came over me about going home for the night. A good friend Terry Wangari had driven from Calgary (three hours away) and she was going to spend the night in Medicine Hat with us. I must admit this was very comforting. Eventually, we decided that Ngala would spend the night with Kefa while Terry, the boys and I went home so that we could be refreshed and go to the hospice early the next day. Later I started second-guessing myself, but decided that it was best that I went home. So, I left specific instructions to be called and the nurse on duty assured me that she would call me as soon as anything changed. Since I had established a routine with Kefa every night before I left, I prayed over him, kissed him, and whispered to him not to leave me. I felt a quiet calm that all would be well.

That was a very challenging night for me, but with all the exhaustion of the day, I quickly collapsed into a deep sleep with my alarm set for 6 a.m. I wanted to be at the hospice by 7 am as usual.

Wednesday, December 19th, 2018 dawned and I woke up early. The first thing I did was to look at my phone and see if there were any calls or messages from the hospice. I breathed a sigh of relief seeing there were none.

For some strange reason I felt a deep peace come over me that morning. I had my morning devotion and read a verse from the Bible that spoke so directly to me. The message, in a nutshell, was about not being afraid when all around seems so overwhelming, scary and uncertain. It was God reassuring me that He was in control of the situation and I did not need to fear death nor what life would be like from then on! It was as if He was telling me to release Kefa to Him and that He was going to take care of the boys and me. I said a bold prayer asking God to give Kefa a peaceful transition into his presence whenever that would be, and to give me the strength I needed to face the day.

I quickly got myself ready and tried to get the boys up as well. They took a bit of time getting ready and I was too impatient to wait. Thankfully Terry graciously stayed with them and drove them over after their breakfast. I was at the hospice by 7 am, anxious to see Kefa and hear how the night had gone.

When I saw Kefa that morning, my heart dropped. I was secretly expecting some improvement, but I did not see any. In fact, the nurse on duty told me it was just a matter of time. We just needed to be around him.

Ngala was up and said that he hardly slept that night. He mentioned that Kefa had not moved the whole night and had some trouble breathing. However, the nurses had drained the fluid build-up and he was able to breathe better.

Ngala stepped out of the room to allow me some time with Kefa alone. I began to clean him up with the help of the health care aides. I shaved his beard and washed his face so that he was ready for the day. Then I sat next to his bed and began playing some messages from my phone, that family members had sent for him. Not long after that, he started gasping for breath. I panicked and rang the bell for the nurse to come in.

Then somehow, I knew it was that time. As the nurse hurried in, the boys and Terry were right behind her. The boys rushed to Kefa's side and we all cried as we watched Kefa take his final breath. The time was exactly 10:10 am. It was hard to believe. We knew it would happen but we were not really prepared for this. Seeing Kefa's body laying lifeless signaled to me that it was over. All my fighting for his health, his life, his healing. It was all over. I wasn't sure what to do next.

One thing I was grateful for was that Kefa had waited for us to come that morning. It was as if he wanted us to be together when he was departing. I consoled myself by saying that was his way of saying goodbye. I hate to imagine what I would have done if he went while I was not by his side. So truly, God was in control. He had given me peace that morning. He answered my prayer and gave Kefa a peaceful transition into His presence.

We gathered in his room while the nurse called our Pastor Jamie McDonald from Hillcrest Church. The nurse told us that we could stay in the room as long as we wanted and that they would not rush us out. Some more friends came by and we cried together. He was not going to suffer again in his body because of that ravenous cancer. Yet even though we knew this was Kefa's ultimate healing, it was not what we hoped for.

Kefa fought a good fight, he ran his race and he kept his faith in God even when it was so dark. We remain confident that he is in the presence of God and one day we will see him again.

We gathered with some close friends and our pastor to forge way forward. We agreed on a funeral home and next steps to be taken. Regarding his final resting place, we as a family decided that Kefa's remains would be interred in Kenya, his home country.

And then began the journey to lay him to rest.

A Time to Rest – Ecclesiastes 3:1-8
Kefa Oduor Tuju

Kefa Oduor Tuju

13th September 1971 to 19th December 2018

Over the next four weeks, the journey to say farewell and give Kefa an honorable send-off flowed as follows:

Monday, 24th December, 2018: Visitation and Viewing at SAAMIS Memorial in Medicine Hat, Alberta, Canada

Family and friends gather for viewing to say farewell in Medicine Hat

Thursday, 3rd January, 2019: Celebration of Life Service at All Saints Cathedral, Nairobi, Kenya at 2 pm.

Family and friends gather for Kefa's celebration o Life Church Service in Nairobi

Saturday, 5th January, 2019: Interment, Ralingo Village, Asembo, Siaya County, Kenya

The boys leading in giving Kefa an honorable send-off in Asembo

Final farewell funeral service in Asembo

Friday, 18th January, 2019: Memorial Service at Hillcrest Church, Medicine Hat, Alberta, Canada

Loving friends celebrating the life of Kefa at Memorial Service in Medicine Hat

EULOGY

On January 3rd, 2019, on a beautiful warm day in Nairobi, Kenya, friends, and family gathered to celebrate the life of Kefa Oduor Tuju at the All Saints Cathedral Church. This tribute is a family perspective of Kefa. We do recognize that he lived a rich life among friends and colleagues in the neighborhood, church, school, extended family, and other associates. This tribute cannot therefore describe the great impact that Kefa had in the lives of the many people he interacted with throughout his life. We pray that you will understand.

Kefa was born on 13th September 1971. He was the beloved husband of Loyce Christine Wangui Oduor, and the father of Jonathan Igeria Oduor and Matthew Tuju Oduor.

Son-in-law to Miriam Wamucie Igeria and the late Amos Igeria Konye.

He was the son of the late Henry Odiyo Tuju and Mary Odiyo and Rispa Odiyo. He was the thirteenth born in a family of twenty-two children, including Raphael, Allan, Anyango, Tito, Ruth, Odhiambo, Roselyn, Awino, Benta, Sila, Collin, Ida, Omondi, Ngala, Betty, Akinyi, Caro, Buore, Pascal, Leakey, and Dana.

Kefa grew up to be a resilient and creative boy, full of humor and aggressive in his endeavors. Kefa joined Madaraka Primary School in Nairobi in 1978 and Khalsa Primary before joining Upper Hill School in 1986, where he also sat and passed his KCSE exam, enabling him to join Kenyatta University, where he studied and graduated with a Bachelor in Education degree. He later enrolled for Masters degree and graduated at Nairobi University with an MBA.

His Early Life

Kefa was a stickler for rules, and did not miss a chance to remind siblings or friends how things should be done. He was always smartly dressed, with polished shoes and clothes ironed. There were a few exceptions though. In primary level, he played football with passion in games that could last three to four hours at a go. He participated in creative sports like gymnastics and loved creating toys with his hands.

Kefa gave his life to Jesus Christ in 1988 while in high school, and stayed in Him the rest of his life. He attended Community Presbyterian Church (CPC) as a young boy till his adult years. He was active in church where he served as a Sunday School teacher, as well as ushering and running weekly fellowship meetings. He, together with Christine who joined him when they got married, found a strong faithful community in CPC, many of whom are still good friends to date. In 2006, Kefa and his family began attending Mavuno Church, where they continued to grow and serve in various ministries in the church (Mizizi, NDOA and LEA) until their transition to Canada. While in Canada, he quickly settled into Hillcrest Evangelical Church, where the family attended and became active in various ministries, also offering leadership in Life Group.

Family Life

Kefa met his beloved wife Christine while at Kenyatta University in 1992. Their friendship slowly evolved into a serious relationship. Two years after graduation they got married on 5th December 1998. Kefa was a caring and loving husband and sought to do all he could to protect and cherish Christine and their relationship. Kefa and Christine were blessed to celebrate their twenty-year anniversary on December 5th, 2018.

Kefa and Christine were blessed with two wonderful boys. Jonathan Igeria Oduor was born 17th September 2000 and Matthew Tuju Oduor was born 16th September 2004. Kefa was a loving and actively present dad who dedicated himself to giving their boys the best that he possibly could, many times going over and beyond. He took time to work through their academics with them, patiently teaching them skills for mastering various concepts they were learning. He instilled a high sense of value for education, inspiring them to aim high for careers that they would enjoy and reap from.

Kefa was determined to give the boys every opportunity they could get to develop their talents and abilities. Over the years, he enrolled them in different activities such as soccer, roller skating, music, drama, and basketball. Not only was he committed to taking them to these activities, but on several occasions took an active part as a parent supporting coaches and participating in parents' activities. At one point he was voted "Most Active Parent" in the Cheza Sport Soccer Club. He even took up learning how to roller skate in his late 30's as he took the boys for their practice sessions. Occasionally, he and the boys would go roller skating at the park together. These were memorable times of bonding with them.

As a Christian, Kefa took spiritual leadership at home seriously. Not only did he take his family to church but took time to pray, read and teach them the Word of God at home. He modeled what a Godly father looks like, fiercely loving while gently disciplining to keep his sons in shape. He encouraged the boys to study God's word daily. He was active in engaging them in activities that would build their faith and connect them with other children in the same journey. Kefa encouraged the boys to participate actively in Sunday School and youth while at church. He was an active parent in the Bible Quizzing program for children at Hillcrest Church.

Throughout his illness, Kefa's biggest concern was for the boys. One of his biggest disappointments was that he could no longer drive them to or be present at their activities. The boys were very understanding and did their best to continue their endeavors to keep his dreams for them alive. Though they were no longer able to fully participate in some of their activities, they continued to do well in the few that they could. They tried to cheer him up by adorning his room with medals they collected with every season of success in both school and in their extracurricular activities.

His Career and Vocation

Kefa began working at ACE Communications Ltd soon after graduation from Kenyatta University in 1996 as a Client Service Executive. In 2004, he opted to venture into a new industry and joined SDV Transami (Group Bollore) where he worked as a Client Account Executive. Despite this being a new industry to him, Kefa set himself to learn the ropes quickly and excel. He began to handle more tasks and was soon assigned one of the company's key clients, Unilever Kenya, where he was seconded to sit and work from. He also decided to boost his education by pursuing a Masters degree in Business Administration from the Nairobi University. In 2009, he resigned to go into business alongside Christine at Floral Interiors Limited. In 2010, Kefa acquired the family business ACE Communications, where he had worked earlier, hoping to kickstart it from its then dormancy.

In 2014 he took up an offer for a position as a marketing consultant at The Dari Restaurant, where he worked until July 2015. Kefa distinguished himself as an honest, loyal, and hardworking employee, winning himself favor with not only his employers but with most of his clients.

After transitioning to Canada in 2015, Kefa was fortunate to get a part-time position briefly as an instructor at the Medicine Hat College, where he taught a marketing course in the winter semester. Kefa loved marketing and this job, though only part-time, gave him a deep sense of challenge and satisfaction.

Kefa was employed by the Medicine Hat School District 76 in November 2015. He was stationed at the George Davison School where he taught English as a second language to children who had recently relocated to

Canada. He enjoyed working with children and many of them attest to the positive impact and influence he had in their lives. He worked there until his passing.

Strengthening Sibling and Family Bonds

Kefa loved his siblings and extended family members. He also settled well into the Igeria and Kibuka families (in-laws) and was loved by all members. He made time for family gatherings and many times was the designated 'camera-man' as he was known for his love for photography and videography. Thanks to technology and the latest communication applications like WhatsApp, he strived to maintain meaningful conversations with those who lived abroad. Kefa was known to bring unity in his family and strived to make peace with all members even where there tended to be normal family feuds. He always cheered everyone with his jokes and boisterous laughter, making him a joy to have around in almost every family gathering. More recently, he was concerned about the rich Tuju family and history that had not been documented. He took the initiative to draw up the family tree, asking important questions and going back to past generations to discover their roots.

Illness

In September 2017, Kefa began having tremors in his left foot. These continued to increase in occurrence and made him weak, forcing him to seek medical attention. On November 20th 2017 a CT scan revealed a mass-like growth on the right side of his brain. He was airlifted to the Foothills Hospital in Calgary where he was scheduled for surgery. After successful surgery on November 28th, 2017, he woke up to the terrible news that he had what was called Glioblastoma Multiforme Grade 4, an aggressive form of brain cancer.

With complete resection of the tumor, there was renewed hope that radiation therapy and chemotherapy treatment, which was to follow, would result in total healing.

Kefa underwent the two therapies successfully at the Tom Baker Cancer Centre in Calgary, and was able to return home to Medicine Hat (Alberta,

Canada) after six weeks. The plan was to continue treatment with monthly oral chemotherapy at home. At the same time, he began rehabilitation through physiotherapy in order to help him get back on his feet.

After a couple of rounds of chemotherapy, consequent scans revealed a recurrence of the tumor and further treatment was put off. The prognosis given was very poor and Kefa was referred to palliative care in Medicine Hat.

All through his visits in and out of hospital, Kefa remained cheerful, hopeful, and positive. He engaged all the staff, whether nurses, doctors, health care aides or porters, in friendly conversations, always finding a point of connection with them. Doctors and staff at the Foothills and Tom Baker Cancer Centre said he was one of the most positive and cheerful patients they had seen. His attitude was remarkable and helped him get through not just the rigors of six weeks of radio chemotherapy but another year since diagnosis.

In September 2018, he was admitted to the St. Joseph's Home, where he continued to receive 24/7 palliative nursing care. He soldiered on, fighting with every breath he had. He particularly looked forward to going home over the weekend to spend some time with family away from the facility. Though it was a risk and challenge to get him home, those moments were profoundly fulfilling, special and memorable to him and the family.

Despite the ravaging effects this disease had on Kefa's mind and body, he never lost his hope and confidence in God to heal him. If healing was not granted, he knew that to die in Christ would be his gain and as fearful as the thought of death was, he was ready to be with his Maker in heaven.

Kefa Oduor Tuju passed away gently in the presence of his beloved family at 10 a.m., the morning of 19th December 2018.

Kefa has won the battle; he is free from pain and suffering!

> "I have fought the good fight, I have finished the race, I have kept the faith."
>
> 2 Timothy 4:7 New International Version (NIV)

His Memoirs

At the end of August 2018, while admitted at the Medicine Hat General Hospital, Kefa felt this burning desire to start writing his memoir, documenting his legacy and history. His greatest desire was to leave a legacy for his boys and the generations to come. He wanted them to have a deep personal relationship with God first and all the rest would follow.

Despite the challenge of his motor function, he was able to type a little and write with his right hand, jotting down key points and ideas. Later, friends came alongside Christine to complete the manuscript by the first week of December 2018.

Kefa was relentless in his desire to complete this memoir and have it published quickly. He specifically indicated that he wanted it ready and published before Christmas of 2018. Thanks to Jim Burk, a dear friend and esteemed author, he was able to offer technical support and publish a copy of the first manuscript as an e-book on Kobo. Kefa was able to live to see his dream come true. This brought an immense sense of achievement and fulfillment to him.

Still, he desired to see the book published in other formats, a project we promised we would do after Christmas and the New Year (2019) break. Little did we know that Kefa would leave us before Christmas 2018. Now that project is underway.

What better way to honor Kefa's dream and his legacy than to purchase his memoir entitled "My Life, My Legacy" by Kefa Oduor Tuju.

"The memory of the righteous is a blessing."

Proverbs 10:7a NKJV

Tributes from His Wife and Children

Christine Wangui Oduor

    This is a tribute to one who was my husband, my confidant, my business partner, my co-worker in the service, my priest, my co-parent, my partner in this journey called life, Kefa. I am still in shock as I grapple with the fact that you are not with us nor are you going to return. I long for you and my eyes are weary with tears that will not dry up. I feel like I am being ripped apart and it hurts!

Kefa, you left too early; this was not in our script as a family!! I am angry that cancer snatched you out of our lives, that you will never live to see all your dreams come to pass. Kefa, it is hard to let you go, yet because you go to a better place, I surrender to God's ultimate will. For in Him, you are eternally healed!!

I will never forget when I first set eyes on you way back in 1992 in Kenyatta University, standing tall, dark, and handsome in blue jeans and a jean jacket. Interestingly, I was drawn to you as a genuine friend, not knowing what would come later. You stood out from among the rest because of your alluring smile and personality. I loved hearing you speak the French language with your classmates and this inspired me to improve on the little French I knew. I am so glad you became my friend, that you saw beyond color, culture and tribe accepting me for who I am. With time you became a friend whom I could confide in and wanted to spend the rest of my life with.

Our common interests became a unifying factor in our relationship over the years, enabling us to socialize, participate and serve in many ventures together. I loved watching you take leadership at home, in Life Group, NDOA, LEA and other various areas of our lives.

I sincerely thank God for keeping you alive to see our 20th anniversary on 5th December 2018. I know it meant a lot to you, even though you were not very strong that day. You braved through the snow to give us a celebratory dinner at your favorite restaurant. I know we have gone through many challenges over the years, but one thing for sure is that this illness strengthened our resolve to be steadfast to our vows. Never have the words "in sickness and in health" taken on such deep meaning. Being your caregiver for the past year may have taken a toll on me all around, but it has also made me a stronger person, more resilient in the face of adversity and more confident in the God who holds our lives in His hands.

Kefa, your signature smile and gentleness was evident to all. I miss your hearty laugh and witty sense of humor that lightened up our home and the lives of many who came into contact with you.

Kefa, you supported me through life as only a true friend could have, encouraging me to work "hard, but mostly smart", and, to do my best. You allowed me to be me, to pursue the dreams and aspirations that I had for my life and career. You supported my big desire to change careers and transition to Canada, choosing to take a leap of faith in your career as well.

You taught me to look on the brighter side of life, always staying positive and worrying less. Your favorite Bible verse was Philippians 4:6-7 NIV which says, "Do not be anxious about anything but in every situation, by prayer and petition with thanksgiving, present your requests to God. And the peace of God which transcends all understanding, will guard your hearts and minds in Christ Jesus." Kefa, you lived a life of peace and confidence in God and I admired that. Even through your illness, you never complained but endured everything despite deep grief and anguish over the struggles you faced daily. I knew you were determined to beat this and come out stronger. You told me that your mum Mary was your biggest inspiration, a woman who exemplified strong resilience in the face of great challenges all through her life. You pressed on, saying that if Mum could make it then you could pull through as well.

Kefa, honey, you were the epitome of true humility. No task was too low for you. You interacted freely with all from different backgrounds with no prejudices. You served effortlessly in various capacities at home, work, church and in the community. I will never forget how you taught me to make 'ugali' while at the university, because this was an important dish for you. Many times, you stepped into the kitchen to clean and cook 'chapatis' among other dishes for us.

Kefa, you were a wonderful father to our boys, going over and beyond to give them the best for a good quality of life. Right from the start you were there, rubbing my back during labor, reminding me how to breathe and finally receiving our boys in the delivery room. You fed, bathed, and nurtured our babies when they were little. You ensured that our home was a clean and safe environment for them to grow up in. I cherish the way you made French our 'secret' parent language when we did not want the boys to hear what we were saying. Many times, you included some of their friends in their fun activities, becoming a mentor to other young boys. Even from your sickbed, you remained active and present in their lives, wanting to know how they were doing and reminding them how much you loved them. You gave them wise counsel for life at every stage. You have left them a legacy that they can continually draw from. Although they need you terribly at this critical time of their lives, I am confident that God their Father will ensure they receive the fatherly counsel and support they will need to mature into godly young men who walk with, and serve God.

Kefa, you were a good friend to many, including your own siblings. You made me comfortable among your larger family when we first met and every moment, we interacted with them. You also formed respectful friendships with my family members, workmates, and neighbors, many of whom will attest to the friend you became to them. Your friends became my friends and my friends became yours, too. Your outgoing personality made it easier for all of us to interact with new people both in Kenya and Canada.

Kefa, you made decision-making in our family so much smoother. While I dillydallied many times, weighing pros and cons, you made urgent decisions with ease, using your God-given counsel and insight. Though we have made mistakes over the years, these too, have been opportunities for us to learn, and, did not tear us apart.

You were a risk-taker in many ways and willing to take on ventures without fear of failure. You always saw the positive in everything and looked at why things would work out as opposed to why they wouldn't.

Our transition to Canada was one of the toughest and most risky decisions we made, and, was not without ups and downs. Paradoxically, it was after your diagnosis and consequent treatment that you were able to fully appreciate why we had to make the move.

Kefa, we will never understand why you came down with such a horrible, incurable cancer that 'seemingly' sapped the very person you were, including your actual life.

One thing we know for sure is that you were right where God wanted you to be. He made you a blessing to many not just in Kenya but also in Canada within a very short time.

We all may not understand why the Lord allowed you to leave us when we needed you most. Though gone physically, your memory will be treasured and cherished in the hearts and lives of many who knew you.

Though it's difficult to see now, I am comforted in the fact that God's ultimate will shall prevail for the children and me. I am so proud of you for taking on the arduous task of writing and publishing a memoir within such a short time. Indeed, you are not gone, as long as your story lives!

The Lord gives and the Lord takes. Blessed be His holy name. May God continually be glorified in and through your life story.

Kefa, my honey, I will always love you. Rest in the arms of Jesus.

Oriti jaherana. Ti warom kendo! (Good bye my love, till we meet again!)

Jonathan Igeria Oduor

Dear Dad, I see more of you in me every day that goes by. That is probably the greatest gift I could ask for. You were the first male figure in my life. Even though you set the bar pretty high, you showed me an amazing example of what a true man ought to be like. I pray that God grants me the strength to live up to the legacy and path you set for Matthew and me.

You left too soon, Father; it's hard to take it in. I still have so much to live up to. Every day I'm learning. I may never be you, but I can be the best me for you. I'm going to become the final product that you tried to produce.

I remember you said to me one day that you wanted me to take care of Matthew when you leave. I promise you once again I shall do that as long as I live.

I cannot imagine what Mum is going through. She is most definitely the strongest woman we know. She fought by your side and now that you're waiting for us in heaven, I will give her the rest she deserves. I will remind her how beautiful she is for you, and I will continue to hug her when she's happy and when she is hurting.

There's never going to be enough to say. So much is still left unsaid. I guess the more suspense, the more we cannot wait for you to receive us in heaven. You kept your faith through the turmoil and the pain. You smiled through the battle and your encouragement to everyone you crossed paths with was not in vain. As you said to me once, "It's not what you take with you when you leave this world, it is what you leave behind you when you go."

I have immense respect for that, because, you definitely left an amazing print on this earth and anyone will agree.

Thank you for the time you spent with us.

Thank you for the sacrifices you made for us.

Thank you for the love and compassion you have for us.

Thank you for being the man who showed us what it is to be a man.

This is not "goodbye", this is more of a "see you soon!"

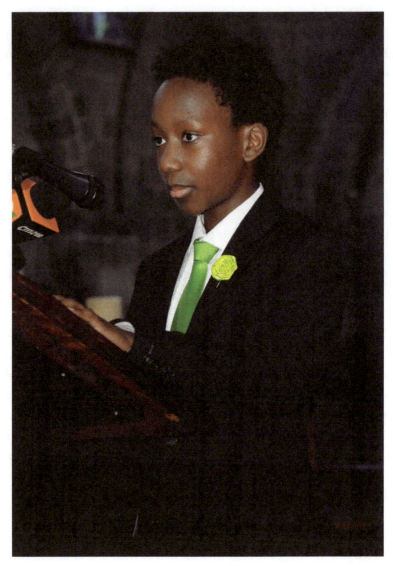

Matthew Tuju Oduor

My dad was the most loving and friendly person I knew and I'm pretty sure everybody who knew him would say the same. He was warm, friendly, and never afraid to talk to anyone, even if they didn't want to talk. He always put a smile on others' faces and, as well, always had one on his. Even through the rough times he always stayed strong and was full of positivity.

It truly is sad that he had to leave so soon because as he told Jonathan and I, he really wanted to see us grow up, graduate, work, marry and see his grandchildren.

I loved his company and enjoyed his stories about life. Just talking to him was a pleasure and honor. I hated it when I would annoy him in my playfulness, because he would sometimes call it out, but really, all I wanted was his attention.

He set a high standard as a father and a husband to my mother, and I pray that I will be able to live up to that one day. I wish he lived with us longer so he could give me more tips on teenage-hood and adulthood because of how wise he was. I just wish I could say 'I love you' to him one last time. I'm proud to be his son and always will be.

We miss you and will see you in heaven, Dad!

OTHER TRIBUTES

His Siblings

Caro
You encouraged me to express myself in English instead of Dholuo all the time. You spurred me on to attend Sunday services at CPC.

When the trumpet shall sound, I know I will meet you there with King Jesus; so, for now, I say painfully but confidently: See you later, dear Oduor, and thank you!

Ruth
I have known and loved you as long as your lifespan. You are one disciplined, humble, brave, witty, and focused soul. I count myself very lucky to have had you as brother, uncle, and admirable father. Farewell, dear.

Ida
When I think of Kefa, I think of loving, focused, determination, bravery and above all God-fearing. May the Lord's perpetual light shine upon you, dear brother.

Dana
You always made family gatherings fun. Thank you!

Achieng
Kefa was a loving person with a great sense of humor. One significant gesture I will always remember him for is that when "baba ma David" required blood transfusion, Kefa was among the first three people to donate blood. We will miss Kefa. "Nind Mokwe" (Rest in Peace). To Christine and the children, may the Lord comfort you and give you strength.

Christine Adem
I will remember Kefa for his LOVE… and will always think of him as living in the hearts of those he touched. We will forever miss you, Kefa.

Allan
Kefa was a gentle man, kind-hearted and above all a peacemaker. We will miss you dearly, brother. May God rest your soul in eternal peace.

Betty
Kefa was a loving, faithful and caring brother, husband, friend, and son. He served others most of his life. He will be missed.

Dan
Kefa, my dear brother, when you were joining standard (grade) one at Madaraka Estate Primary School, I was a senior in the school. Our parents gave me the responsibility of taking care of you and to see that everything was well with you. It was fun and joyful taking care of you. You were an obedient, hardworking, loving, highly responsible and God-fearing person. We will miss you very much, my kid brother. Fare Thee Well.

Akinyi
I will miss you dearly, my loving brother. My strength lies in the assurance that you've gone to a better place.

Bebi

We came to your house in Langata and South B for birthday parties and played on the bouncing castle. Memories of you driving us home to Asembo for family get-togethers are clear in our minds. You put us together at our grandma's place to watch movies. It was very exciting being with all my cousins. We miss your care and love for children. R. I. P.

Pascal

Our citizenship is in heaven, from which we also eagerly wait for the Savior, the Lord Jesus Christ. Blessed are those who sleep in the Lord. You are a blessed citizen of heaven, bro.

Omondi

Every stage of my childhood, you were there. Knowing and discovering life and things almost simultaneously and in adult life you converted many of those life lessons to your rich legacy. Setting for siblings a benchmark of legitimacy and authenticity. Well done, Dwodi. You are now healed forever!

Sila

In Galatians, we read that the only thing that counts is faith expressing itself through love. Kefa lived a life of faith that expressed itself through love. To God be the glory!

Ngala

Kefa taught me many things I did not have before: patience, humility, life skills, to mention a few. He was born and I came right after him. When he died, I kind of died too. Actually, he left this world on the day that I was born. I have never felt such a void. We differed sharply on issues but we maintained respect for each other. He was amongst the best listeners of our time and he listened to the end.

His In-Laws Pay Tribute

<u>The Igeria Family</u>:
With his stunningly disarming smile, Kefa strode into our lives through our sister Wangui when he was a young university student. Even then, he was a gentleman who loved the Lord and blended high standards with great humility. He cared deeply for all his family members and friends. His amazing sense of humor endeared him to everyone. Indeed, with Kefa, you were always guaranteed a good laugh. Ever dependable and available to all who needed him, Kefa always put others' needs before his. With his very positive attitude towards life, which he exhibited even to his last days, his calm disposition and strength of character, Kefa left an indelible mark in each person who was no doubt privileged to meet him. He was a deeply committed Christian, which was evident by his devotion to his dear wife and sons for whom he was always a pillar of strength. Though he constantly thanked us for giving him a wonderful wife, it is we who are eternally grateful and honored to have had him in our lives. We celebrate him and his many unforgettable qualities, in the knowledge that he is now in a happier and better place. We will miss him unbearably as he has left a huge gap in our family. Rest in Peace our brother, son, uncle, and dear friend Kefa, till we meet again!

<u>Our Grandmother, Loise Wangui Wamaitha Kibuka:</u>
Baba Jonathan was a great blessing to us. He loved us and I loved him dearly. But now that he is gone, it is I that shall go to him. Our God is a husband to the widow and father to the fatherless. Let us put our trust in the Almighty God. From Cucu (Grandma) Loise.

<u>Dr Dan and Betty Gikonyo and Family:</u>
Kefa came into the lives of Gikonyo's long before he became an in-law.

It all began on a fine sunny Sunday afternoon at our home in Lavington. It was a special day as our American friend, Maria, wanted to use our garden to record a video of her Afro aerobics dance. We had selected our friend, Raphael Tuju, to take up the assignment. His team manager was none other than Kefa Oduor, his brother. He was on a pre-university job with his brother, Tuju. An amicable young man with a broad contagious smile who laughed easily and heartily. Little did we know that several years later, he would meet and fall in love with and marry our beautiful niece Wangui.

He was a loving person, affable, and was great company.

Wangui, Jonathan and Matthew, you are blessed to have had a gift like Kefa for the years God had predestined. As your family we shared the love and hearty laughter that was his hallmark.

May God and the choir of Angels continue his welcome into the heavenly choir.

Veronica Kebuka and Family:
Kefa was a lovable, dependable, and delightful friend, son, and fellow believer in Christ. He walked in humility, gentleness, and genuine love towards all—especially the family, guided by an unshakable faith in Christ. I watched him diligently teach this faith to his sons with a deep conviction. I and my daughter's family will miss his friendliness, positivity, genuine laughter, kindness, and generosity. We shall meet again!

Dr Gethaiga and Sheila Kibuka and Family:
"You cannot measure the height of a tree until it has fallen." – a Ghanaian proverb

When Kefa Oduor came into our family, we realized how easy it is to love and live with other different ethnic communities. We saw his love, humility, respect and care for others, cheerful heart, godliness, and strong values for the family institution. Kefa had begun building bridges a long time before. Raising his boys, Matthew, and Jonathan, with these priceless values, we are confident his legacy will live forever. May the Lord rest him in eternal peace and comfort Christine and the children.

Timothy and Wambui Gitonga and Family:
Kefa, you were an example of a fine young man. Your smile says it all. It was an honor knowing you and knowing the love you had towards your wife, Wangui, and the boys. You became part of the Kibuka family and though we loved you, God loved you more and that is why he called you home. In the end, it's not the years in your life. It's the life in your years that counts. You

will be missed by all. Our prayers are with Kefa's family and the entire Tuju and Igeria families.

<u>The Kiragu Family:</u>
Sometimes painful things like these happen; Kefa has gone before us. But even here God remains God. We have no words to express our deepest grief. We loved Kefa. To us, Kefa is the miracle and angel that God sent to our family. We recall him in his beautiful smile, a kind word and embracing love. We loved him as a son, dad, uncle, cousin, and friend. It pains us deeply, beyond grief, that Kefa suffered an incurable illness and has rested before us. Even here God remains God.

As Christians we draw our faith from our Heavenly Father and we are secure in our Salvation through Jesus Christ. While these certainties remain, we mourn the loss of Kefa, our loved one. At this time, we turn to God to comfort our sorrows and we comfort one another with 1 Thessalonians 4:13-18. Because of the Resurrection we are assured that the Lord Himself will descend from heaven with a shout, with the voice of an archangel, and with the trumpet of God. Those dead in Christ, including Kefa, will rise first. Then we who are alive will be caught up together in the clouds to meet the Lord in the air. God remains God.

Bible Verses

1 Corinthians 15:50-58 New International Version (NIV)

50 So, I declare to you, brothers and sisters, that flesh and blood cannot inherit the kingdom of God, nor does the perishable inherit the imperishable. *51* Listen, I tell you a mystery: We will not all sleep, but we will all be changed— *52* in a flash, in the twinkling of an eye, at the last trumpet. For the trumpet will sound, the dead will be raised imperishable, and we will be changed. *53* For the perishable must clothe itself with the imperishable, and the mortal with immortality. *54* When the perishable has been clothed with the imperishable, and the mortal with immortality, then the saying that is written will come true: "Death has been swallowed up in victory." [a]

55 "Where, O death, is your victory?

Where, O death, is your sting?" [b]

56 The sting of death is sin, and the power of sin is the law. 57 But thanks be to God! He gives us the victory through our Lord Jesus Christ.

58 Therefore, my dear brothers and sisters, stand firm. Let nothing move you. Always give yourselves fully to the work of the Lord, because you know that your labor in the Lord is not in vain.

1 Thessalonians 4:13-18 New International Version (NIV)

Believers Who Have Died

13 Brothers and sisters, we do not want you to be uninformed about those who sleep in death, so that you do not grieve like the rest of mankind, who have no hope. 14 For we believe that Jesus died and rose again, and so we believe that God will bring with Jesus those who have fallen asleep in him. 15 According to the Lord's word, we tell you that we who are still alive, who are left until the coming of the Lord, will certainly not precede those who have fallen asleep. 16 For the Lord himself will come down from heaven, with a loud command, with the voice of the archangel and with the trumpet call of God, and the dead in Christ will rise first. 17 After that, we who are still alive and are left will be caught up together with them in the clouds to meet the Lord in the air. And so we will be with the Lord forever. 18 Therefore encourage one another with these words.

Psalm 23 New International Version (NIV)

1 The Lord is my shepherd, I lack nothing.

2 He makes me lie down in green pastures, he leads me beside quiet waters,

*3*He refreshes my soul. He guides me along the right paths for his name's sake.

4 Even though I walk through the darkest valley, I will fear no evil, for you are with me; your rod and your staff, they comfort me.

5 You prepare a table before me in the presence of my enemies. You anoint my head with oil; my cup overflows.

6 Surely your goodness and love will follow me all the days of my life, and I will dwell in the house of the Lord forever.

Psalms 92:12

The righteous will flourish like a palm tree, they will grow like a cedar of Lebanon; planted in the house of the Lord, they will flourish in the courts of our God.

Kefa Oduor Tuju was laid to rest in his rural home of Asembo, Nyanza Province in Kenya on January 5th, 2019. The whole journey to his interment was one of solemn celebrations of his life; he was honored in life and was also honored in death. He will be forever cherished, loved and remembered by many. We are so grateful for the opportunity to share life with him and are confident that we will meet him again in heaven.

And so, it is we who fulfill his dream to have this memoir published once again after his passing on, knowing full well that though he is gone physically, his legacy lives on!

"The story of a life is a priceless legacy." – Linda Spence

Kefa Oduor Tuju resting in eternal peace

Forever in our hearts

ACKNOWLEDGEMENTS

Many people have had an impact on my life over the years. It is not possible to acknowledge them all. I offer my most sincere apology to all those I may have missed. I send my most sincere appreciation to the following people for being part of this journey, my life!

Pete and Joanne Rose
Nicholas and Hellen Langat
Ngala and Judy Odiyo
Marcus and Evelyn Coneys
Ken and Lynn Klym
Pastor Jamie and Carrie McDonald
John and Felicia Adegbenjo
Joely and Joe Augustino
Joe and Conny Grove
Marvin and Carol Salazar
Brad Dilman and Family
Ron and Sandra Rude
Life Groups in Hillcrest Church
Hillcrest Church Family
Donna Serr
George Davison Elementary School Staff
Nikki and Todd Johansen
Emma Piayda
Petara Panabaker
JP and Aaron Boodhoo
Reagan Weeks

Rev. Lisa Waites
Lisa and Lucian Stanescu
Tom and Purity Kimani
Bahati and Chris Thom
Damaris and Joseph Mutua
Kenyans in Calgary
African Community in Lethbridge
CPC Madaraka Church Family
Wasafiri/Warriors Group
Mavuno Church Family
LEA Teams in Kenya
NDOA Group in Kenya

PHOTO GALLERY

Celebrating my 26th Birthday with Christine in Jamhuri Estate, Nairobi, 1997

Celebrating our 10th wedding anniversary, 5th December, 2008

With both mums, aunt and siblings in Nairobi, Kenya, December 2008

With Aunt Janet and siblings in Nairobi, Kenya, December 2008

Walking with Matthew for the Heart to Heart Foundation in Nairobi, Kenya, 2013

At the shores of Lake Victoria with Dad, year 2008

Visiting with 'Cucu' (Grandma) Loise in Kenya

With Christine's siblings, nieces and nephews, December 2014

With my sweetheart facilitating our LEA meeting at Mavuno Church, 2015

With the boys at home in Nairobi, Kenya, July 2015

Arriving in Amsterdam, August 16th, 2015

Having fun at the Gun Hub in Medicine Hat, Alberta, 2015

Celebrating Father's Day in Medicine Hat, June 2016

Finishing Water Run with Christine and Nicholas Langat in Medicine Hat, Alberta, October 2017

Made the 5km walk in Medicine Hat, AB, October 2017

With my dear friend Ken Klym, December 2017

After surgery with Jonathan, December 2017

With my great son, Matthew, 2018

With my great son, Jonathan, 2018

Last family portraits taken in July 2018, lovingly donated by Petara Panabaker Photography

With the love of my life, Christine, July 2018

*Last family portraits taken in July 2018,
lovingly donated by Petara Panabaker Photography*

Lightning Source UK Ltd.
Milton Keynes UK
UKHW021105250221
379301UK00008B/152